Praise for Reality and Hope

To me, Reality is joy, pain, happiness, and sadness. It is reflection and self-awareness. To me, Hope is a belief that every dream will become real. Thus, Reality and Hope is the balance we need.

– Daryl W. (Calabasas, CA)

Reality and Hope is a spectacular collection of small passages that will change the direction of your life. No matter what life is throwing at you, you will find insightful and inspiring ideas in this book to help you move forward. Don't miss this book.

– Chris H. (Enola, PA)

Like many people, I find that my day-to-day decisions are often more instinctual and subconscious than I would like. *Reality and Hope* brings perspective to my chaotic life by sharpening my focus and helping me pause and consider the choices I make on a daily basis.

– Mike R. (Draper, UT)

Reality and Hope is a valuable resource, providing insightful guidance for navigating through daily triumphs and obstacles. Steve's thoughts motivate self-reflection and action. This book will inspire you to own your life on your terms.

– Mark R. (Plano, TX)

A great way to bring balance to one of the toughest aspects of life: how do we remain hopeful while staying grounded in reality?

– Tom J. (Walnut, CA)

Reality and Hope adds light and clarity in a world full of darkness. It doesn't take much to get off track today, and having something so clear, simple and truthful helps validate my purpose. This should become a daily discipline to assist in living a better life.

– Sean M. (Lake Oswego, OR)

Black vs. White. Good vs. Evil. Grace vs. Truth. Realty vs. Hope. This book will help guide you through the biggest challenge you will ever face: how do I live a spiritual life on earth in this human body? Steve's insightfulness will help lead the way.

– Lewis H. (Timonium, MD)

The ability to communicate the reality and hope of every situation is a fundamental skill for those looking to positively impact the people they lead and serve. These writings will challenge you, stretch you, and provide a road map for your personal and professional growth. I highly recommend *Reality and Hope* to everyone, from the sales professional to the CEO.

– Dan F. (Newberg, OR)

Reality and Hope has had the uncanny ability to provide a fresh drink of water when my heart was most thirsty. It has helped me to reframe my thinking, encouraging me to either face the circumstances head on, or to see them in a new light. May this be so for all readers!

– Christine J. (Arvada, CO)

I hope you will sit back, relax and be in the moment as you read *Reality and Hope*. Steve teaches us through his wise words to stop, slow down, and listen to gain perspective on our current Reality. I hope this book will arouse in you — as it did in me — a greater love for yourself and others.

– Sarah M. (Littleton, CO)

We all face trials in our lives and business. This book speaks to a variety of them and reminds me that there is a fine balance between where we are, and where we really need to be focused. *Reality and Hope* is a shot in the arm when we need it most, with lessons for our everyday challenges. It inspires me in times of trial and reminds me why I'm really here. This book speaks to my heart by offering both grace and truth.

– Carrie G. (Burnsville, MN)

REALITY AND HOPE

Reflections from a Coach's Chair

STEVE SCANLON

2nd Edition: Copyright © 2016 by Steve Scanlon. All rights reserved. No portion of this publication may be reproduced, stored in an electronic system, or transmitted in any form or by any means, electronic, mechanical, photocopy, recording, or otherwise, without the prior permission of the author.

Published by: Red Lizard Press.

Scripture quotations used by permission from the New International Version. Used by permission from Zondervan Publishing House. All rights reserved.

Quotes by Jim Rohn, America's Foremost Business Philosopher, reprinted with permission from Jim Rohn International ©2011. As a world-renowned author and success expert, Jim Rohn touched millions of lives during his 46-year career as a motivational speaker and messenger of positive life change. For more information on Jim and his popular personal achievement resources or to subscribe to the weekly Jim Rohn Newsletter, visit www.JimRohn.com.

Library of Congress Control Number: 2015959383

ISBN 978-0-9970174-0-3

Reality and Hope: Reflections from a Coach's Chair / Steve Scanlon

Printed in the United States

Photo Credits:
Pages 5, 45, 68, 95, 109, 137, 157, 173, 189 - Allie Harkavy
Pages 1, 25, 83, 121 - licensed under Creative Commons

This work is dedicated to my faithful colleagues at Rewire, my former colleagues at Building Champions, and to the thousands of clients who have inspired me throughout my journey as a coach, speaker and workshop facilitator. Without their dedicated efforts and noble actions, I would have nothing from which to reflect and give back.

May these reflections re-ignite your flame.

Contents

Foreword by Wil Armstrong

Warm and sunny is how I remember the day in June several years ago when I strode into the doctor's office for my annual check-up. I thought I felt fine and life seemed good to me. I had no reason for alarm. By the time I came out, however, my world came crashing down on me. The confident stride I had walking into my appointment was now slower and measured. I received news that no one at 37 ever thinks you'll hear.

In my early teens, doctors discovered I had a heart murmur. It was pronounced enough that you could hear it by putting your head on my chest. But I never thought too much about it because it never slowed me down. No restrictions were ever put on me. But in the course of just a few years between check-ups, things had changed.

My heart had enlarged and was now laboring with a leaky mitral-valve. The prognosis was not good — heart attack, stroke, or even death. I needed open heart surgery to fix it, and we had to do it fast.

I remember the days before my surgery wondering about my new reality. Was I going to make it? What would happen to my family if I didn't? Would I ever be the same again? Looking back on this defining moment in my life, it's funny that I didn't think about the next big deal or the work sitting on my desk. My present reality offered me something quite different.

I turned my thoughts to new hopes while trying to embrace what was going on with my body. Would I grow old together with my beautiful wife or dance at either of my daughters' weddings? Would I be strong enough to come home and play a game of catch with my son? These were the things that grounded me as I entered surgery and throughout a long recovery. I thought a lot about reality and hope.

I first met Steve Scanlon in college where we were both studying business. He was a gregarious sort who had a zest for life and a knack for making people think, feel a bit uncomfortable, and laugh all at the same time.

Over the more than twenty years that we've been close friends, I've seen him live out his faith and work in demonstrable ways that offers people something different. With his family or in business, Steve has been all about reality and hope. He's the real deal. Unfortunately, most people along the way come to believe that hope fades and reality is a synonym for disappointment. Steve has a different story to tell.

Reality and Hope may seem on its surface to be "a riddle, wrapped in a mystery, inside an enigma" — to paraphrase Winston Churchill. That's exactly where Coach Steve wants you. Yet he brings his best thinking from years in coaching to Reality and Hope with crisp anecdotes, humor, and a passion uniquely his own. Steve offers us a tonic that goes beyond soothing the mind to warming the heart. As only a coach can, he leads us through these pages to grasp our real existence and connect it with our desire to make things better. Read on!

Wil Armstrong
Denver, Colorado – May 2011

INTRODUCTION

Irrespective of what challenges or darkness may come, the light wins in the end.

Introduction

The book you hold in your hands is a collection of works that represent the ideas, strategies, and tactics that are a result of coaching individuals one-on-one over the span of many years.

Like so many authors before me, I had a strong desire to write a book around the concept of hope alone. I am bent toward wanting to see the world through fun, good, and hopeful lenses. The truth is that there are also plenty of "realities" that impact us all. By embracing those realities — rather than conveniently avoiding them — we may actually accomplish more and become the people we are truly supposed to be.

The title "Reality and Hope" comes from a lesson that I taught in Vermont to a group of people that I used to coached and who met quarterly. It was a simple lesson based on a question so ubiquitous that most of us don't think of it very meaningfully.

The question is, "How are you?"

What I proposed to that group — and what I am proposing to you today — is that when you hear that question and prepare to answer, you quickly create a simple dichotomy in your mind: Reality and Hope.

This idea was born out of the words of F. Scott Fitzgerald:

> *The test of a first-rate intelligence is the ability to hold two opposed ideas in the mind at the same time, and still retain the ability to function. One should, for example, be able to see that things are hopeless and yet be determined to make them otherwise.*

As you will see in the pages ahead, while reflecting upon coaching sessions with my clients, I have endeavored to face reality head-on while still offering hope. For the record, I do not think that Reality and Hope are opposing ideas. Rather, I believe that they go hand in hand.

During my years as a coach, I learned so much, and am so grateful that life-long learning was a part of what we did. I have learned that it is very human to want to stand on one side of a fence, and difficult to accept that there may be two sides (or more) to any given topic, field or endeavor. Reality and Hope is, I believe, a blending of the sides rather than a division.

Truth be told, the reality side of things is impartial. It doesn't just represent the negative in life. Reality is reality, and it is very possible that your reality today is hope-filled. It is also possible that your reality finds you in a tough season. Either way, reality should be embraced wherever it is.

Should we endeavor to live a complete and fulfilled existence, then we need to drink deeply from both reality and hope. It is my desire and my prayer that this book gives you a glimpse of both sides — if "sides" are even how we want to see them.

This book is not meant to be read cover to cover, but rather in "snippets." We have broken down the "snippets" by theme, so you may choose to open to a chapter that describes what your soul thirsts for today.

In the process of reviewing the book, I noticed that I tried to end each page with a hopeful thought, often some action that we can take that will bring us to a better spot. If there is one overarching theme that I have observed, it is this: irrespective of what challenges or darkness may come, good wins.

My life and my vocation stand as personal testimonies to the fact that hope, love, faith and goodness win in the end. We need reminders of this, because seasons of darkness — however real — must eventually give way to the light. My ultimate hope is that the pages ahead will help you feel connected to the realities of life while still offering you the life-giving hope we all need.

I wish you well on your journey. May you be richly blessed along the way.

Never deny reality. Never lose hope!

Steve Scanlon

EXECUTE WITH INTENTION

Be one of the few who can declare that they do, indeed, have a plan.

Make Your Plans

Go sit down and write out your plan. If that were ordered of you, how would you respond? What happens inside your mind or in your heart when you are asked to make a plan?

Perhaps some respond favorably, but many, many others recoil and would just as soon get a root canal. Thus, the vast majority of business professionals simply don't (or won't) make the time to have a written plan. There was a mythical study done on Harvard graduates regarding those who made plans versus those who didn't. The study, allegedly done in 1979, looked at the difference in success (measured by income) between those who had a written plan for their future versus those who did not. Quite predictably, the ones who had a plan made far more money.

Now, we know that money is not the only gauge of success, but the point was to highlight just how few had written plans. Did Harvard really do this study? No one seems to know. The point, however, is not hard to follow intuitively. Harvard or not, we can easily accept that making a plan works!

The funny thing is that almost everyone who hears about this study believes it. Not because it is attached to the name "Harvard," but rather because it just makes sense. I have recounted this study in front of groups of people several times and it always comes with head nodding as if to say "yep, we know we would be much more successful, regardless of how we want to define our own success, if we took the time to have a written plan."

There are a few reasons people don't plan, but I am just going to list this one: fear of failure. It's not that we don't know how or even that we don't see the benefit. We simply fear the pending failure of not measuring up to our own judgment when it's plainly written in black and white.

I beg you to fight through your fears and write down your plans. Don't get suckered into thinking that not having a plan is the surest way not to fail. Most of us have found the opposite to be true.

Prophesy Fulfilled

Recently, I attended a meeting at my 11-year old's charter school. The administrators had rallied as many teachers and parents as they could to tell us that our little school was on the ropes. The financial realities of our community and our school district have made it very difficult for the school to stay alive.

As I listened to their appeal, it struck me that many people are struggling to eke out a living. Then, the meeting took an odd turn. The principal of the school began to speak about what she believes the school will look like in five years. She gave an amazing and vivid description of what the school will become. She drew on past experiences to prove that this is where the school will go. She then invited a couple of parents to talk about their kids who had attended this fledgling school years before, and who went on to pursue college degrees and are leading happy, healthy lives. I was stunned. I have heard pleas for funding before, and I wasn't expecting this outpouring of vision and belief. And yet, the current reality was not ignored. Reality and hope.

Common people can do uncommon things in challenging times if we simply believe that the future has something good in store for us. You do not have to pretend that difficulties don't exist in order to believe you can achieve great things. Are you in a tough situation that requires you to both recognize the difficulty and embrace a new future? Is it possible that you are actually in a great situation, but you are surrounded by those who are struggling? Either way, as a coach I simply cannot overemphasize the power of articulating a vision in difficult times. I have no doubt that our little school will make it. But the truth is that, if the principal had shared only the current reality and pointed out how dire things were, I wouldn't have given it much of a chance for success.

Are you giving others around you such Vision? I hope you are. If you are only pointing to the difficulties and only seeing the current day's challenges, you may very well be a part of a dark self-fulfilling prophecy. This is the very essence of Reality and Hope. Let's live it.

Stuck in a Moment

Should I focus my energy and effort on all that is in front of me right now, or should I spend time planning for the future? This is a timeless issue that is rearing its ugly head in a big way. For so many people in our country, this is a time of great scarcity. It is times like these that accentuate the need to both work hard every day in our existing role and spend some time planning for the future. This may not be the most earth-shattering thing you have heard all year, but like so many other timeless truths, it is one thing to understand the truth but a whole other gig to put it into play.

Right now, many people are stuck between knowing that they must follow a vision, and just getting through the day. The truth is that tough seasons call for us to do both. It is what Jim Collins — in his work *Built to Last* — referred to as the "Tyranny of the Or". Great companies, like great people, learned not to ask "should we do this OR that?" but rather acclimated to the idea that they needed to do both.

You may need to dust off your vision and update it, rejuvenate it or fully re-write it. People die without a clear vision. You could ask King Solomon or Viktor Frankl (were they still alive). Without knowing in our heart where we are going and why, all our work may be futile. But we must work, and work hard.

I am totally hip to the concept of "work smart not hard." But today I think we need to work hard, put our heads down and put the hours in. Of course you should be smart, that is a given. But if you find yourself stuck asking if you should be envisioning and planning or executing and working, the simple answer is "both."

Imbalance

Life balance. Has there ever been a more oxymoronic pair of words? Is it really possible to have balance? The concept of attaining balance in life is somewhat controversial. Some say it is possible and others argue that it will never happen. Some claim that balance is becoming proportionally less possible as our lives become increasingly convoluted.

If work/life balance means that every component of your existence is in perfect harmony at all times, then I agree that balance is improbable, if not impossible. This is one reason why I have coached people through the process of a creating a life plan. Not necessarily because having one will get you to some fictitious place, but rather because a life plan will afford you the opportunity to make corrections on the long and winding road.

Most people will never write a life plan. Most people these days would argue that they don't have the time. Stop and consider that for just one second: most people won't make the time to create for themselves a plan that would invariably lead them to make better decisions about their time. Really?

If Gary Larson were still drawing cartoons, that would make a wonderful *Far Side*. If you are feeling particularly out of balance, writing a life plan would be a great step for you. No coach will promise that it will solve all of your challenges, but at least you'll have a framework for better decisions in your life. The best case scenario is that you will live more intentionally. I do not believe that we will ever achieve perfect balance on this side of eternity. I do believe, however, that living intentionally with a plan in hand is instrumental to our peace and prosperity.

Making Time

"Time Management" is an oxymoron. No one can manage the ticking of the clock. We can, however, manage our choices during those ticking hours. Too often we get sucked into thinking that some days just happen to us. How many mornings do we wake up with a plan, only to look up at 5 o'clock and wonder where the day went?

It always sounds so pleasant to talk about managing our days more effectively, but the truth is that it requires gut-wrenching intentionality. If we are going to accomplish what we set out to do, we must control what we say "yes" to, and what we say "no" to.

If your life feels uncontrollably busy, it is possible that you need a solid dose of "On-Time." On-Time is the art of stepping away from what you do every day to evaluate WHAT you're doing and WHY you are doing it. It enables you to get your bearings, to see the big picture, to evaluate and make corrections before diving back in. I can't think of a single person I coach that hasn't benefitted from some good On-Time.

The problem is that the people who need On-Time most don't believe they have time for it. How's that for irony? It is unfortunately very common to make yourself so busy that you no longer take the time to consider how to better approach your day, your challenges, and your opportunities. As a result, your day is less organized, your challenges are more daunting, opportunities are missed – and the busyness multiplies.

If you are one of the multitudes caught in this destructive cycle, it is time for you to courageously break free. Put a solid block of On-Time in your calendar, and treat it like you would a very important meeting with your best client. Some of you will need a few hours, and some need a day or more. This is not "Off-Time." This is intentional reflection and planning in an environment that will allow you to see the proverbial forest for the trees.

It won't be easy, and initially it may feel unproductive. But stick with it, because it may be the very thing that makes your future days more purposeful and productive. I assure you it is a great investment.

A Simple Plan

As a coach, I believe that success in business and in life results from a combination of blessing, hard work, skill, and timing. Luck has little to do with it. Samuel Goldwyn once said, "the harder I work, the luckier I get." If you subscribe to my definition of success, then there is good news: most of the equation is within your control. You have it within you to work hard and improve your skills. You may not be able to control the timing of events, but you can be ready for them when they come around.

In working with a lot of individuals, I have found business plans to be good, but simple business plans to be better. When I was with Building Champions, we had a tool called the Simple Business Plan. When we offered this plan to business professionals, it was often greeted with a sense of relief — likely because people are so overwhelmed with the complexity of their lives that they long for something simple.

A simple business plan has three components and fits on one page:

Outcomes (or Numbers)

Disciplines

Improvements (or Projects)

I coached through this process for some time and, while the vast majority of professionals admit to having no plan at all, this simple plan is one that anyone can use. If done correctly, it can be an amazing guide for your business.

There are a few simple suggestions about how to nail the numbers, identify the disciplines, and define the projects. But there is no need to overcomplicate this process. Give a little thought to each, put them in writing, and you will have a process that can guide your days and support your priority management.

We invite you to be one of the minority who can declare that they do, indeed, have a plan. Try it. You will see the benefit of having something so simple impact your business and your life.

The Specificity Trap

Most of my clients have heard me clamor about the acronym S.M.A.R.T. Still, it is so crucial to one's overall success in business and in life that it bears repeating. Specific. Measurable. Attainable. Realistic. Time-bound.

This is the filter through which we must put all of our actions if we want the highest degree of success. But I must admit that being specific is difficult. Why? Because the probability of excuse is so greatly diminished when we state our actions specifically. And we cherish our excuses!

When we declare that we are going to take action, and we do it vaguely, we build in our own hand-made loop hole. It is our "out," a fabricated freedom to choose to do something or not. It is kind of like trying to build a home and having blueprints that are only the outline of the house.

Consider the following two possible disciplines that might appear on a salesperson's business plan: 1) prospect more, or 2) make three proactive outbound calls daily to new prospects, and do this every weekday at 10:00 AM.

Now, if you were a person who likes to bet, which of the two disciplines would you bet has a higher probability of execution? It's obvious isn't it?! And yet, so many of us continue to express our actions in vagaries. Once, after speaking to a group of business professionals, I had a gentleman approach me and tell me that he didn't like what I had to say at all! Somewhat shocked, I gingerly asked why. He said that he was uncomfortable stating the disciplines in his life so clearly because it would force him to take action, and he simply didn't like to be forced to do anything.

I was speechless.

Go get specific. Start today (at 10:00). I promise it will help! True freedom is hidden in the success that comes from the seeming bondage of specific action! You can take that to the bank.

Opportunity at Hand

I had a daydream once about writing a book entitled *What I Thought was Opportunity Ended Up Being a Great Distraction.*

I admit the title would need a little work. But it still amazes me that so many of us chase after new projects and goals, believing at the time that they will provide us with amazing results and subsequent freedoms. Often (but not always) these endeavors lead us away from being great at our current roles.

I couldn't tell you how many times I have coached people who go down roads that are not parallel with their existing vocation, only to learn that they would have been so much better served to have keyed in on their current plan.

I suppose that some people get bored and are just looking for something new to do. Perhaps others are just trying to beat the system that calls for discipline and perseverance. In extreme cases, some believe in the 'ship coming in' theory and are convinced that they are one opportunity away from never having to work again.

If any of these describe you, ask yourself if you would accomplish more and get closer to your goals by staying focused and being great at your current role.

I am not insinuating that there aren't opportunities and that from time to time we shouldn't take risks, because there are — and we should. Still, there seems to be a plague going around that causes us to pursue ideas that distract us from hunkering down and being excellent at the job at hand.

There will be some people who read this and grit their teeth at it and defend their right to pursue "other interests." Again, I am not at all saying that you shouldn't. I am simply saying that the dreams and aspirations that we have are often fulfilled, not by some magnanimous occurrence, but through executing the plan we have day in and day out.

Opportunities are there — and most of them are wrapped up in what we call the disciplined life. Be great!

Planting Positive Seeds

You reap what you sow. Consider this ancient piece of wisdom for a moment. How does it apply to your life? When you consider reaping and sowing — the planting of seeds and the subsequent harvest of a crop — do you think something positive?

Quite honestly, this little saying has always carried with it a tinge of negativity for me. I always think of it in conjunction with some negative event, in which I must consider what I did to create the series of events in the first place. Today, I want to invite you to take this quip of reaping/sowing and consider how it can be spun in your world for positive results. What seeds can you be planting today that will yield a harvest of good things in your life?

It takes quite a bit of self-awareness, to consider that all of the actions you are taking in your life today will ultimately produce something. Self-centered pursuits, entitlement thinking and overall scarcity mindedness are seeds that produce a crop of fear and anxiety.

If, however, your thoughts and actions are centered on the authentic betterment of others and the relentless pursuit to care for and love those around you, you will yield something entirely different. The voice out there in our modern world is so loud and so pervasive, that if we are not careful, we will listen and plant crops of entitlement that in turn render vast fields of anxiety and eventual aloneness. Turn against what the world says will bring you health, wealth and happiness and instead pick up and plant seeds that grow others.

If this sounds silly or in any other way unattainable then I beg you to consider what seeds you have in your hands. We must distinguish between good and bad seeds.

May your harvest be plentiful.

Practicing

In the spirit of jocularity, I would like to point out a practical joke being played out in businesses every day. In fact, this practical joke has a much broader reach than just business — it impacts almost everyone I know, including the guy I see in the mirror. Here it is: many of us are so busy doing our jobs that we no longer believe we have the time to practice our jobs. Thus, by our own self-made busy worlds, we impose a rather funky form of mediocrity.

In coaching at Building Champions, we referred to practice time as "On-Time." The idea is to work "on" your business, and not always "in" your business. It's a fairly simple concept, and just about every great athlete has figured it out. I've never heard of a champion golfer who goes from tournament to tournament and just plays. The best of the best spend hours every day practicing and perfecting their craft.

So why don't most business people do that?

One reason is that we are convinced we are too busy working in the business to intentionally work on it. It is pretty simple to see how and why an athlete would spend time working on themselves, but we don't correlate that type of activity with our professions. The practical joke is that the busier and crazier we make our calendars, the less time we have to do anything similar to practicing in our jobs. We may appear to be moving forward. But the glass ceilings we hit and the mediocrity we arrive at don't do anything to help our business, and the wheels on the bus go round and round!

Commit to getting off this insane loop today by courageously blocking time for working ON yourself and your business.

We would be crazy not to take this lesson from every world-class athlete. But if you are reading this and wondering where you will find the time, just know that the wheels can only go round and round for so long before one of them blows out on the highway. On-Time anyone?

The Ultimate Goal

Goals are tricky.

You would think that as a coach I would already have developed strong convictions around the idea of goals. The truth is that, as a result of my experiences with clients, my own ideas seem to be morphing into something different.

For the record, I believe that setting goals is a good idea. I have worked with many people who have not only set them, but have declared their goals in writing and made them specific, official, and public. This can certainly help you achieve something that you may have not otherwise done.

A problem arises, however, when the goal itself is the ultimate objective. If you hit the goal, the question then becomes, "Now what?" People often hit their goals, but don't consider what will come next. Perhaps this is why it is so common to feel empty immediately following hitting an objective. Interestingly, it can feel similar to missing the target.

I would like to propose that goals in your business and in your life should carry less weight, or at least an equal amount, than other objectives that last far beyond any one endpoint.

If, for example, you set out to be the number one salesperson in your company in a given year, you might also declare your resolution to become a more caring and focused individual. Whether or not you win the "prize," you still have something very noble to achieve.

I believe there is much wisdom in having less tangible targets in your business and in your life that will not rise and fall with the completion of a specific event. I suppose that this is yet one more paradox for Reality and Hope.

Goals are good, and I will continue to coach people to set them. But if they are not accompanied by an even greater purpose, they can become a snare.

The New MBA Program

When economic times get tough, many people look to higher education to take their vocations in a new direction. Business people often spend a great deal of time and money getting a Masters of Business Administration — AKA, MBA. To be certain, this degree can open doors and help you in numerous ways.

I would like to propose a new meaning for the letters MBA. If we all adhere this acronym, it could be as life-changing as actually going back to college. From hence forth, I declare that MBA stands for MEASURED BY ACTION.

I have often observed my clients writing fantastic vision-like documents and declaring some really wonderful ideas in their business plans and life plans. Thinking strategically and claiming the future with our words is a powerful way to unearth a new reality and forge new roads. Let us never forget that "without vision, people perish" (courtesy of our good friend King Solomon).

But vision must turn into action. One way to do that is to create MBA's — Measurements. How will you measure along the way?

It is one thing to state that you will "grow your business," "create new relationships," or "get in shape." But we must never forget the power of measuring, and our measurements must reflect specific ACTION. Without an MBA, vision is so often an unattainable dream. If you haven't figured it out by now, we coaches are big on Action. While we know that all great endeavors start with Vision, we also know that it is Action that makes the Vision come to life. So let us all get our MBA's and become people of action. I will venture to say that if you get your higher degree in Measuring By Action, it will reward you more than any MBA Harvard ever offered.

Make Good Picks

If someone forced me to choose a single adjective to most accurately describe people's lives and businesses today, I would have to go with "overwhelmed." It is impossible to compare different seasons of life, and therefore futile to try and decide if this particular one is more overwhelming than seasons past. Nevertheless, the sheer amount of activity coming at us these days is, well... overwhelming.

Much of our success, our joy, and our peace is contingent on our ability to make good choices in this season. I would also venture to guess that the choice to take certain actions (or not) is more crucial in compressed times.

As a coach, I deal with people's decisions daily. What are they picking? To go here or to go there? Respond to this or that? React to this situation or that one? Be reactive or proactive?

These picks happen all day, every day. If you have dialed business, vision and life plans, all of your picks get put through this filter of your own making. When these strategic documents are not in place, then you are much more likely to make your picks based on how you 'feel' in the moment.

Here's the rub: if we are always making choices based purely on how we feel — and we all admit that we are feeling overwhelmed — then we must step back and realize that our own picks may disserve us. Let us be very cautious about a season in which feelings can be extreme. When we feel like we're riding an emotional roller coaster, then our choices will be random and possibly dangerous. It may be a great time to step back and re-evaluate where you currently are and where you are going.

If you are one of the multitudes who feel they don't have time for this, I want to encourage you to see that taking this time to stop and reflect could be one of the greatest time savers you ever choose. As you reflect and plan, you will make better, more intentional picks in the future — not ones based solely on the emotion du jour. This, in turn, will get you closer to your objectives and save you hours of cleaning up the mess of bad choices.

Time On

How can we make the most of our days? How can we ensure that we are hitting our disciplines, adhering to our plans, and being efficient with our time? This seems to be one of the most commonly travelled quests in business and in life: The Road to Improved Priority Management.

There is an ancient Greek word "Kairos" that is translated as "making the most of every opportunity." This is good advice, but this pursuit can also be a trap. In my time as a coach, I have seen too often that people will pursue accomplishment and activity, without giving any value to stopping and thinking. I am guilty of this as well.

Our world esteems activity and accomplishment so much that we have dismissed the idea of taking time to slow down and simply think. "What a waste of time," we declare, as we quickly move to the next project, the next email, the next step in the plan. The coach in me knows that steps and plans and implementation are crucial. However, as the world spins faster and information spreads at the speed of light, there is even more reason for us to step back and reflect on WHAT we are doing.

At Building Champions we referred to this time away as "On-Time" — taking the time to work ON your business and your life rather than just incessantly IN it. Where in your day, your week, or in your month are you putting this kind of time in your calendar? I believe that you simply cannot make the most of your opportunities if you don't take some On-Time. But know this: if you build it into your day, the world around you will say you are foolish. Interruptions and urgency will feed your nagging compulsion to spring into action. It feels good to keep moving, even if you are just spinning your wheels.

If you believe you have no time for such a thing because you are so compressed with activity, then I am speaking directly to you: It is when you have the least amount of time to dedicate to On-Time that you need it the most.

Don't Look Over Your Shoulder

"How are other people doing?" This is a question that coaches are asked every day. It is so human to want to compare ourselves to others. I just can't find any merit in it. If you compare yourself to someone else and you find yourself better, it will lead to pride — the kind of pride that comes before a fall. If you compare and find yourself lacking, it can lead to a lack of confidence, depression, and a whole host of other problems. If you must compare, then compare yourself to your own possibilities. In the Beijing Summer Olympics of 2008, Jamaica's Usain Bolt shattered the record for the 100-meter foot race in an amazing 9.69 seconds. In the last 10 meters, Bolt broke every cardinal rule of racing by arrogantly lifting his arms in celebration as he looked over his shoulder to see where he was relative to his competitors. Yes, he broke the record and won the gold medal. But immediately, the announcers and spectators realized that he could have finished even faster if he had just kept his eyes on the goal.

Let's stop looking over our shoulders. Let's keep our eyes fixed on our own goals. Forget about your competition. It is quite likely that they are looking over their shoulders at you. When it comes down to it, there are two key problems with looking over your shoulder in a race.

It can negatively impact your psyche. Sports psychologists and world-class coaches have proven that the psychological benefit you think you'd get from knowing you are being chased down is not nearly as powerful as the one you can get from believing you have what it takes.

It slows you down. When you turn your head and shoulders to the side you create drag and lose precious microseconds. That goes for your life and business as well. Don't jeopardize momentum. Keep your head and your eyes fixed on your own tape. The likelihood that you will win increases greatly when you don't allow yourself to compare.

Look at the Map

Creating a yearly plan for your business in December or January is a common occurrence. Reviewing, revising, and following that plan mid-year is not so common.

As the months go by, many people stray from their business plans. I want to remind you of the power of reclaiming your plan.

If you are going to take a long road trip, you don't plan out your route and then lock the map in the glove box. You refer to it frequently, to get your bearings along the road so that you don't get lost. This is precisely why the best of the best get out their business plans and re-commit on a regular basis.

There are many ways to write business plans, and you may have your favorite. But the world around us is so dynamic that your plan can quickly become useless if you don't read it and apply it often. That's why a one-page plan is so useful — it's much easier to keep it front of mind as you plug along through the year.

So, where are you at with your plan? Are you on target? Are there any trends in the numbers that would be useful if you studied them? Being conscious of trends is one of the most powerful reasons to continue to adhere to your plan.

What disciplines do you need to amp back up? Specific, measurable disciplines are a crucial component of any plan, but many of us grow weary over time and simply need to recommit. Do you need to rejuvenate your goals? Have you hit what you said you would? Some of my clients have exceeded their goals and need a bigger challenge to keep them fired up in the fourth quarter as a result.

For some, the review and update of their plan is going to be a reminder of a fruitful year. This can add some wind in the sails. For others, it is a reminder to get back to the things that they know will help them finish the year stronger.

So what are you waiting for? Get your plan out and make these days your best yet.

The Perfect Plan

Ready, aim... ready, aim... ready, aim... go back and make sure you are ready.

This is the unintentional and sad thought process for too many people who wish that discipline were more a part of their everyday lives. Too many times, I have caught clients trying to make their plans perfect rather than getting out and giving what they have. This often presents itself when a client asks about a particular script or approach to a new prospect. I would venture to say that there may be no such thing as words so golden that you don't feel some sense of awkwardness when speaking to someone for the first time. Sure, we can be polished and articulate, but more important by far, is that we simply pick up the phone or go to that meeting and give what we have — warts and all. As a coach, I am all for a solid plan, but in the spirit of trying to possess a 'solid gold' plan, some people never take the simplest of steps to start executing that plan.

There is a great saying that goes something like this: "the half-baked, imperfect plan you execute today is infinitely more effective and meaningful than the perfect one you never do." Truth be told, our perfecting ways are often a mask for our well-developed call reluctance. The good news is, this is curable. If you have fallen for the "ready, aim" conundrum, stop waiting for the perfect words or situation. Take that little step. Stop aiming. Fire!

TAKE ACTION

All of your goals and ambitions may be in vain without taking the small, seemingly insignificant steps

Back and Forth

"The longest journey you will ever take is the 18 inches from your head to your heart." This is one of my favorite quotes and one I have been thinking about for many years. The quote itself can seem quite ethereal and vague.

The truth is that when we lose heart — or when our heart is not in the right place — all of the head knowledge in the world may not help us achieve any of our goals or dreams. Taking this head to heart journey is paramount to one's overall success. What I am learning, however, is that the journey is not a one-way road. The journey seems to be one that is back and forth from head to heart and from heart to head.

Action happens when our minds are made up about a matter. Certainly you can will yourself to some amount of action even if your heart is in the wrong spot. But your actions are much more likely to succeed if first you make the journey to understand your heart's position, and then come back and engage your mind.

The Apostle Paul wrote "Do not conform to the pattern of this world, but be transformed by the renewing of your mind." (Romans 12:2) In a single verse I believe he captures the essence of this heart-head journey. Paul is writing about transformation (heart) and clearly a different "mind" set.

If your heart is right, then it is time to go and take action.

If you feel mired by inactivity and in any way hindered in your ability to go in a specific and actionable direction, you may just decide to stop and take the journey into your heart. This may include spending time in prayer or meditation, going on a vacation where you can rejuvenate, or perhaps writing (or re-writing) your life plan.

Never forget that everyone you encounter is somewhere on this path — so be gracious.

The Final Step in Any Process

Over the course of my journey as a coach, I have created many processes, systems and structures that are all intended to help others execute on their ideas. I have created most of these as a result of observing how many clients implemented really well and many, many others that did not. I can't help notice that there are a few commonalities in those who struggle to implement. As I work through the first few stages or steps of any process, I lay out what I believe are very tangible and practical instructions that would help you take big and small ideas to completion.

Today I want to tell you about the final step.

The last step is always and simply entitled, "Execute." Now, some of you may be thinking, "Well... Duh!" But what I have found is that so many of my clients would swiftly and meticulously move through all other steps and still not pull the trigger. Every coach has moments when we have to kick in with higher accountability to help our client go the final mile. I can't begin to tell you how many people – especially dominant type personalities — have drawers and shelves stacked with projects that are 90% complete. If you've been guilty of this, it may be time to pull those unfinished projects out of that dusty drawer. You may be surprised at how close you are to completion.

You very well may have a great process yourself for getting done all that you need to. You may have read a bunch of books on the topic or emulated someone else who did it well. Irrespective of what your process is, the last step must always be "Execute". In this sense, Nike is correct.

Small is Big Enough

I am a Forrest Gump type of runner — I just run. Maybe one day I will stop in the middle of a run and quit forever, wondering what the point ever was. In the meantime, I run to be alone, I run to pray, and I run to get ideas. On a recent run, I was thinking about simpleminded analogies between running and life. It struck me that often in life, we miss the little steps.

We have learned so much about the big picture and goal setting that often we get too caught up in it. But most often, the success we have in almost any endeavor is because of the simple steps we take, and not just because we dream up some lofty goal.

Sure, I believe in the power of having those goals, but all of the great goals and ambitions in the world will lead you nowhere without the small, seemingly insignificant steps.

If someone in your life forced you to pick between being a great goal setter and being a great small step taker, pick the latter. You will go further. Sometimes in my own disconnected life I think everyone should be a runner. Mostly because I think everyone can. If you want to be a runner, start by walking around the block. Do it for a week and then go a block and a half.

Dreaming of a marathon may actually disserve you. Most of us are not ready for a marathon today, and the distance to be overcome may cause you to quit before you begin.

Start with the simple steps. You will learn that anyone who ever became great at anything had to walk that same path.

Lean In

I sometimes catch myself coaching a few clients to "lean in" to certain situations. At one point, I had to stop and consider why this phrase kept coming out of my mouth the way it did — and what I even meant by it. After a bit of soul searching, I have come to a better understanding of this euphemism and how it can help us. By "lean in" I mean "to go against the grain and do something that you wouldn't normally do in order to improve your situation."

When you lean in, you make that call you would rather not make. You go out and visit that person you would rather avoid. You reach out to a friend or a client in an unexpected way in order to make their life better. The simple fact is that almost every one of us has some deeply ingrained habits that are tough to break.

I remember being at a conference where the presenter asked everyone to put their watch on the other wrist while he presented. He then went on to prove the point of how we cherish little habits, and how uncomfortable it is to do even the little things that are outside the norm.

Leaning in to a situation means getting uncomfortable and allowing yourself some freedom to do something that you wouldn't ordinarily think to do. My recommendation is to do this specifically where relationships are concerned, and only do it if it's an action that somehow improves the recipient. Don't do it just to do it. You can switch your watch just to prove how uncomfortable it is, but it doesn't really benefit anyone.

Leaning in is about more than just doing something — it's about improving. Lean in this week. Take an action, something simple you wouldn't normally do. I have no doubt that all of us need this discomfort from time to time.

If it is Worth Doing...

GK Chesterton, the famous British philosopher, stated that "if a thing is worth doing, it is worth doing badly." I often find myself coaching a client to implement a sales strategy that inevitably relies on their willingness to pick up the phone or meet face-to-face with one of their customers. It becomes a game of tug-o-war as I keep pushing the client out the door (so to speak) to actually make the sales call.

It is a strange form of call reluctance when people keep trying to make their approach perfect. They want to use the best words, have the best approach, and essentially do everything possible to take away any element of fear and anxiety from selling. This is why Chesterton's quote is so perfect. In the end, we may simply have to face the fear and make those calls. They may be less than perfect. You may fumble through the words. Your material may never be exact. And from time to time, you may even be bad — but it is worth doing even if it is difficult. What in life, of value, isn't? In the end, it comes down to conquering fear. Recently, my friend Carol handed me a sheet of paper with the word fear as an acronym. Fear, she wrote, stood for Fictitiously Envisioning an Action's Results.

In other words, we are projecting a negative outcome before we even attempt the action. Because of that negativity we often don't take the step to be with people. Just remember — the half-baked, poorly executed plan will always beat the perfect one you never try. Take action!

Frog Swallowing

I was recently at a business event where the topic of procrastination came up. It is something that seems to plague everyone from time to time, and some people have it at a stage five level. If you have suffered from this disease, read on — and if you put off reading it until later... well, I guess you'd better find the nearest swamp.

There is a saying about swallowing frogs which recommends that you do the thing you least like quickly, so you can move on to what is more palatable.

A good friend of mine explained that the derivation of this comes from Old England, where it was once thought that the secretions of certain toads cured specific ailments. But even back then, the thought of swallowing a toad really didn't have much appeal.

The story goes that people would put off the cure until the disease got so bad they had no choice. A toad (or frog, or some type of amphibian) would be tied to a string and then swallowed. The secretions from the toad's skin would then be ingested, and the dead animal pulled back out.

Perhaps at this point, you are actually gagging up a little bile. I hope so. The allegory of "first swallow the frog" comes from the idea that the ancient physicians would tell patients that procrastinating would only make their disease worse.

So, what do you procrastinate? Is there something that would be good for you, that you don't enjoy doing, and you put off again and again? Don't wait until the only cure is to swallow a frog. This disgusting tale is designed to instruct us to take action, and take it quickly. Putting the right things off is as bad as bile.

Out of the Ruts

"The only difference between a rut and a grave are the dimensions." Ellen Glasgow's quote is a fascinating concept to consider. We all get into ruts — some are small, some huge. The good news is that there are ways to break out of these trenches we occasionally find ourselves in.

The first thing we need to do is come clean about the fact that we are responsible for carving the path that made the rut to begin with.

It is only after we declare this fact that we can begin to step out. A rut may be something as simple as a repeated pattern of inaction in your daily life — those calls you need to make, the letters that need to be written, the books yet to be read — something you simply put off. If done long enough (also known as procrastination) you have successfully developed a rut.

I have noticed that the human mind has unlimited capacity to explain and justify our actions (or in this case inactions) but you can do that till the cows come home — you are still in a rut. Some ruts can become trenches or deep chasms. Others are well-worn pathways that we have created, and it is possible to escape.

Perhaps you are hoping I will give you some mystical, out-of this-world answer for how to get out. The simple truth is that after you claim responsibility for the rut, you can then choose to declare a different course of action. You will need to accept that the action will go against your grain and against your reason — and that takes courage.

Nothing takes greater courage than to battle your own self-made justifications. You have to admit that you were wrong and then be willing to do one or two small things that make you very uncomfortable. You don't need a new life, you don't need a lobotomy and you don't need to be excessive. Today, take one small positive action that you wouldn't normally take in the face of your challenge. It is amazing how you can dislodge yourself from a rut by following this simple step.

Cheers to more even roads — out of the ruts!

Action and Faith

Often we must take on disciplines that do not give us an immediate payoff. In fact, one key reason why more people don't live a disciplined life — at work or at home — is because the actions we must take to achieve a certain objective are often followed by a period that forces us to patiently await the results.

If, for example, you believe that making five proactive outbound calls each day to people in your sphere of influence will render positive results, you must also know that those calls very often don't render anything — today.

It is so tempting to believe that doing a certain thing will immediately produce a specific result. When we don't get it as quickly as we would like, we simply stop taking the action.

Action, if it is not followed by faith, causes most of us to stop taking the very action that would have likely produced our desired end result.

There are many definitions of the word 'faith.' For our purposes today, let's go with: 'belief in something that does not rest in logical proof or material evidence.'

The world in which we live pounds into us the idea that, if you put forth any effort, you should get something from it instantly. If we have inadvertently subscribed to this theory, then it could be that our false expectations have held us back from achieving great results.

There is no promise that the positive actions you take will render anything immediately. Highly successful people understand this and take action anyway.

It is time to take that leap of faith.

Slay Your Shoulds

Busyness is overwhelming for so many people right now. There are just too many of us who are missing important areas of our lives because urgency has taken over.

As we pile on more and more, the word 'should' rears its ugly head in our hearts and minds. I should work out more... I should go out with my wife more often... I should take a small vacation... I should wake a little earlier and spend some time in prayer and meditation... I should put down my iPhone and be present with my kids... I should be more disciplined in my sales efforts.

The list of 'shoulds' is quite extensive. So extensive, in fact, that it's just easier to ignore all of it and simply allow all of the busyness to happen to you. Or... you can kill your 'shoulds.'

My recommendation is that you not look at all of them collectively at first. It may seem so overwhelming that it causes you to turn away from it entirely. Instead, pick one 'should' and kill it. You needn't even begin with the #1 'should' in your business or life. You may spend so much time trying to decipher which one is most critical that inaction inevitably occurs. Just go at one — any one — today. Make that 'should' a 'do.'

There is little in the world so empowering as taking action against a 'should.' Momentum is built around small steps in our businesses and lives. Then, as momentum builds, you can surgically go after more and more of them.

We all have 'shoulds,' it is part of life. There are some who choose to address them head-on, and as they do they experience greater and greater freedom. We construct our own self-made prisons when we allow the aspects of our lives that we 'should' do to run rampant.

True freedom is found when we wake up and realize that we have the power to destroy our 'shoulds.' Pick one today and go for it. You will be so glad you did. See you on the momentum train!

Intangible Action

I spend my days with people coaching them to take specific, tangible action. I can't think of a single person who would deny the fact that taking action would positively impact their life. It would be easy to write about tangible action.

Just a little more than 200 years ago, Sir Isaac Newton gave us his three physical laws. While they were meant to explain motion, we can easily see how "to every action there is an equal and opposite reaction" applies to life as much as to our physical surroundings. I doubt I will ever go down in history for creating any such cool laws, but as I considered this empirical truth, I wondered if it couldn't be said that "to every action there is an equal and opposite inaction."

If this is true, then we live in a world where inaction is as prominent as action. This explains precisely why we wake up every day and don't do all of the things that we know we should and could do. Today, I want to encourage you to take the time to ask, "Why?"

Time is at such a premium these days, and we don't often see the value in stopping to question our behavior or evaluate our choices. Consequently, we roll along and allow life to happen, rather than making time to consider the WHY behind what we do and don't do.

To ask yourself WHY takes great courage. In fact, many who started reading this will have discarded it by now because it is simply too difficult. Coaching people to get to their WHY has proven to be the most difficult thing I do. It is resisted with fervor. The courage and time it takes is simply too much for some.

Asking WHY is effectively a journey to get to your heart, and it can be grueling. If the actions (or inactions) you are taking today aren't getting you where you need to go, perhaps you will consider a different path. I hope you do. And if you do, remember that there are people willing to be on that path with you.

Lose heart and you lose everything. Proverbs 4:23.

Anomalies

By definition, an anomaly is an inconsistent, odd, or peculiar situation. It may be surprising to you to know that, from time to time, I have clients — including the guy reflected in the mirror — who do not do what they say they are going to. Yes, I realize that this is a shocker, but it is sadly true. All action plans do not get completed with excellence and on time. We have a strange habit of looking at our lives and businesses as a series of anomalies. Here's how this works: We commit ourselves to some course of action... and then we don't do it. We then tell ourselves that the reason we didn't do it was because of a crazy time during the week, or that it was a terrible time of the year or something happened that almost never happens.

The truth is that "stuff" happens all the time. We must see things for what they really are if we are going to become the people we wish to be. I am all about seasons in life. Things really do happen that are "one-offs" and do not repeat. However, we must all be honest about what is a "season" and what is becoming a "lifestyle." If we observe this distinction, it could be tremendously beneficial in our quest to become people who do what we say we will do.

Let us call ourselves out. If something is truly an anomaly, it is my hope and prayer that you move through it gracefully. But if it goes beyond a season and becomes a way of life, may you call it what it is and take action in a different direction. I am remembering Jim Collin's words when he said, "The signature of mediocrity is chronic inconsistency." I don't know a soul who couldn't use a little more consistency.

Set Straight

Most people agree that, if they would take the actions they know they should, then they would become successful. The actions that most people need to take are not mysterious to them. This begs the question, "Why don't I just do this?" Sometimes as coaches, when we are in the midst of helping a client identify the actions and put them into their calendar, we pause to ask the question, "Why aren't you doing this?"

The "why" question can quickly turn a coaching session into a counseling session. But sometimes, counseling is exactly what is needed.

A good counselor helps you look backward. They help you examine what motivates your behavior for the purpose of uncovering things that are not clear to you on the surface. This takes time and a skilled and educated professional to be most effective. However, all of us can play the role of counselor from time to time, because good counselors are excellent listeners.

We may use some counseling techniques as coaches, but we know our limits. My goal is to get the client back on track, so we can start looking out the windshield again and not in the rear-view mirror. We do need to get back to taking action.

If, however, your mind and your spirit are in a funk, all of the accountability a coach can offer will do you no good until you do something to set your heart right. If you are not taking action, and you know that your heart is in a bad place, you may need to uncover why.

Some people will need to spend quite a bit of time in the company of a good counselor, while others need just a glimpse to set their course straight. Thankfulness is a miraculous tool which can do wonders for your heart and soul. Gratitude and forgiveness can turn your life around and set you on a different path.

My recommendation is that we go deeper than we ever have in this season of life to be thankful. It can only do us good.

The 5% Rule

There is not a single life form on Earth that doesn't face challenges. Problems, confrontations, threats and mis-met expectations seem to be part of everyday life. Perhaps one of the highest levels of enlightenment comes from accepting these challenges, embracing them and owning our part in them.

Fascinatingly, most people simply will not own their small part of the problem. If you think about the #1 challenge in your life today and actually take the time to put it on paper, you may realize that 95% of the problem lies outside of your control. It is so human for us to look at that 95% and argue about it, complain about it and get frustrated on how IT doesn't change. Even if we see the 5% that is in our control, it seems so futile to work on it when we have no influence over the other 95%. Our world will simply be a better place to be, when collectively we look at that 5% and make commitments to ourselves and to others to improve it. If, for example, you have a strained relationship where the other person is 95% in the wrong, you have a choice. You can spend your time pointing out how they are in the wrong or you can spend your time working on the 5%. It may not seem fair, but at least you will be working on the only part of the equation you have control to change. If every one of us would only have the courage and wisdom to work on our 5%.

For those of you who remember the movie *Groundhog Day* with Bill Murray, you will remember with clarity how futile life was when he blamed the world for the 95% they got wrong. It wasn't until he began to accept that he was part of his own living hell that the situation changed.

Let us not repeat that same error. Go own it!

Are You Right?

What we do, what we say, and how we react usually seems right in our own eyes. Even King Solomon said, "All a man's ways seem right to him." (Proverbs 21:2) When we take (or don't take) action, we believe we are "right"— at least at the time. We go to great lengths to justify to ourselves how right we are.

It takes a tremendous amount of courage to look at our actions in light of our desired results, and to concede that we may need to alter our course. Thus, many of us refuse to change direction, because change itself is so frightening. Instead of travelling a new road or considering a new way, we stay put. Then, we look with great surprise at our results and marvel that they are not what we wanted.

Perhaps each of us needs to consider a different path and different action.

Any coach will tell you that if you are not achieving the goal you have in mind, then you need to do something different. You must stop looking outside of yourself and see that it is you that needs to change. Now certainly, we needn't change everything. Many things we are doing every day are pointing us in the right direction, and we are seeing the results. But if you can identify one place in your life or your business where you continue to miss the mark, consider a different path. Change is good. Not easy, but good. Embrace it.

Take A Different Road

Make a choice today to do something different than you normally do. Drive home from work taking a completely different route. Eat something you normally don't eat. Wear something you don't normally wear. Call someone you wouldn't normally call. Any one of these actions could make you uncomfortable, but there is a reason for it.

A little more than 10 years ago I chose to become an executive coach. It was one of those choices in life that didn't seem to make much sense to the outside observer. At one point, I was trying to explain to my father what coaching was and what a coach did. My father was a CPA, and had been for his entire career. Gentle though he was about responding to my decision, it was invariably puzzling for him. I know inside he was thinking I had lost even more of my mind than he had previously believed.

Then, he said something that I will never forget: "Sounds a bit to me like you help people get out of their own way." After a decade of coaching, I don't believe I could craft a better description of what it means to be a coach. We all "get in our own way." And sometimes we do it through incessant habits.

This is precisely why most people don't achieve their potential. They establish habits that are comfortable, and don't let anyone challenge them. Wouldn't you love to break some bad habits? But alas... where to start? You can start by simply changing a few little things that you normally do. You will note the awkwardness and discomfort of doing things differently. Then, if you can do some of these smaller things, perhaps you are up for some bigger changes — the kind that may help you get out of your own way.

Establishing a new habit is as easy to talk about as it is difficult to achieve. My recommendation is that you start with something easy and build from there.

Momentum

Momentum is an indescribable, intangible quality. If you play or watch sports regularly you can often feel the force of momentum swing a game. But what causes it? Is it just a matter of attitude? Does the team or individual athlete do something different? Is it just some random, serendipitous sequence of events that are uncontrollable?

Here's what I have observed about momentum in life — whether it be in your personal life or in your business: positive momentum happens when you decide to execute on an activity that is good for you, but against your will in that moment.

Momentum happens when you do what you should, when you should, whether you feel like it or not. This is the very core of discipline.

As a coach, I get to observe many people gain that mysterious momentum, only to look back and realize that it began simply because they extended themselves to hit a discipline — and didn't stop to ask themselves if they felt like doing it! Furthermore, I have seen that one needn't have momentum in every aspect of life or business in order to really pick up steam. Many times it starts with one simple, consistent act. Try it.

I could also tell you about how momentum is thwarted when one continues to refuse to take the action they know they ought, but for now let's stick with the positive. Today can be the day your momentum changes.

The best way I know to conjure up this mystical force is to act on some simple fundamentals, irrespective of your current feelings towards them. Remember that action creates inspiration — not the other way around!

Advance and Live

In a coaching session once with a great client (I'll disguise his name and call him "CR"), we uncovered the fact that many people in CR's marketplace were just sitting back, waiting to see what would happen this year. Loitering is rarely a good idea in business, and it ain't much of a strategy in life either. I thought about the title "Wait and Die," but instead I went for the other side of the same coin.

Patience is a virtue, and certainly there is a time for reflection. But in many cases, the virtues of reflection and patience are quickly turning into inaction and stagnation.

Today could be the perfect time to re-take the proverbial hill. Get out there, schedule the meetings, make the calls, and recommit yourself to your non-negotiable disciplines. Don't sit on the sidelines! You need to be in the game, playing hard and going strong.

You can always find some prognosticator who will tell you that things are about to get really ugly. The good news is that you needn't participate in the ugliness, and the best way to thumb your nose at bleak predictions is to take action. There has never been a better moment to be excellent at your job. Everything you have ever heard about discipline and "going the extra mile" is in play right now.

The future will wreak havoc on those who don't intentionally choose to advance. But for those who make the choice to take action, the future is bright.

Will you be one?

THE ART AND SCIENCE OF DISCIPLINE

The success of the season that lies ahead of us will likely depend on our own willingness to work hard and smart.

Dreaded Discipline

When I use the word "discipline" as a coach, it is usually met with a general sense of disgust and disdain. Many times, when I find myself speaking about a particular topic (like discipline), I return to the definition so as to not lose the original concept of the word. I believe that one of the best definitions of discipline I have heard is, "to do what you should, when you should, whether you feel like it or not." I want to invite you to consider the "feeling" part of that definition; to do what you should whether or not you feel like it. If you "felt" like taking some specific action and took it, I am not so sure it would fall under the category of discipline. I believe that discipline is about doing the right thing in your business or your life specifically when you do NOT feel like doing it. Almost everyone I have ever met can accomplish the things they are already motivated to do.

Do you want to take some giant leaps in the way of leading a disciplined, fruitful life? Do you have a desire to see your business increase or your effectiveness grow? You may want to consider taking a specific action that you should in times when you do NOT "feel" like doing it.

This concept goes against what the world wants you to think. Most advertisements want you to have what you want because you deserve it and because it "feels" good at the time. This is in direct opposition to the meaning of discipline and frankly what holds so many of us back.

I have seen clients take action specifically in the face of not feeling like it was what they wanted to do. The rewards have been rich and meaningful. So, what aren't you doing, that you should, simply because you don't feel like it? You may only need to come up with one small thing to work on, in order to really get some momentum going.

4 Steps to Better Discipline

There has to be a point in all of our lives when we ask the question, "How can I be better disciplined?" Whether you are thinking about your health, a key relationship, a commitment you made to learning something new, all of us have at least one area where we have struggled with discipline.

Helping people to take action and lead a more disciplined life is what I am all about. In a recent coaching session on this very subject, I identified with my client a quick 4-step process that may be instrumental in helping you with a key discipline in your own life or business:

Step 1: *Get buy-in.*

If you are committing to a discipline, let the closest people in your life in on it. Don't even attempt without the accountability that comes with their knowledge.

Step 2: *Schedule the discipline in your calendar.*

Treat this discipline like you would an important meeting with a key client. I cannot tell you how many times people make commitments only to not put the action in their calendars. If you don't schedule it, it will be too easily edged out by other things.

Step 3: *Be prepared to say NO.*

It's very likely that a new discipline will have to take the place of something you are already doing. At some point, or perhaps every day, you will have to say no to something else in order to sustain the discipline.

Step 4: *Tie it to something bigger.*

When you commit to a new discipline, you must be able to see a connection to something bigger than the discipline itself. Find the connection so your heart is in it as well as your head. Any one of these 4 steps can make a difference in helping you have success with a discipline. When the steps are done together, the result can be transformational.

Go make a difference!

Your Way

Some time ago, Daniel Harkavy and I crafted a presentation entitled "Your Way" for one of the quarterly meetings of an executive coaching group we led through Building Champions. The essence of that lesson was to unearth the little "ways" of doing things which combine to make us successful. We weren't looking for the obvious disciplines, but rather the behind-the-scenes everyday activities that we rarely look at or question in our lives. We asked the group questions like, "How do you awake in the morning and what is your ritual?" "What is the manner with which you go through e-mails?" "What is the last thing you do before you leave the office each day?"

As it turns out, there were great lessons to be learned from examining the things that one doesn't usually examine. To this day, I have many clients in that group who still talk about their "way." Now, there is a catch. Your "way" has a dark side.

While there are certainly some ways that are healthy and helpful, there are also some that have become bad habits. Habits that need to be broken. Perhaps you have a "way" that you go to sleep at night. Your mind is racing, so you stay up late and work. You know you should get out of bed earlier in the morning, but you can't because the bad habit of staying up late has overtaken you.

This is but one example of a "way" that needs to be questioned. The real issue with some of our little "ways" is that we don't question them. They seem so natural, so innocuous. I have challenged some of my own ways, and it has been fruitful — and frankly, quite painful.

If you are reading this and something is popping into your mind about a "way" that you have, it is quite possible that it may need to be examined. My experience as a coach says that when one looks at these things and endeavors to change them, great things happen.

If you have good "ways," exploit them. But if some are holding you back, then I implore you to see the truth and be willing to change.

A Strange Choice

It is true — but perhaps a bit trite — that life is full of choices. One might even say that our cumulative choices make up the very essence of who we are. Success in business and in life is also a choice. Now, there is much that goes into that choice, and it isn't always obvious or easy. If it were, the whole world would be successful.

So here's another odd choice to make: you can choose NOT to have a choice about your daily disciplines, or you can choose to give yourself a choice. Perhaps I should explain…

Many people walk around knowing precisely what they should do. "I should exercise," "I should be home by 6pm," "I should make that call." The problem is that so many people make these activities a choice, and then they choose not to do them. Others set boundaries in their day, and simply don't view certain activities as a choice.

One key "success principle" (if that term doesn't also seem trite) is that, when you get clear about what your non-negotiable disciplines are, you remove the choice. You create an impermeable boundary around that activity.

This makes people uncomfortable. In some weird way, creating boundaries makes us feel as though we are being robbed of our freedom. We live in a time and place where we value freedom — we fight for it and sue people if they don't respect it. This may sound outrageous, but your freedom could be the very thing keeping you from becoming successful.

Boundaries are good when they are the ones you impose upon yourself to keep doing the things that you know you should. When you strip away the choices that allow yourself to wriggle out of your disciplines, then you are choosing success.

Accountability

Accountability is one of those topics that I believe is widely needed, fiercely avoided, and highly misunderstood. What does it mean to you to be "held accountable" to something? If you surveyed 100 people you would get at least that many answers. Whenever I ask a group of people if they believe accountability is a good thing, I inevitably get a resounding "yes." It has always seemed like an odd phenomena that so many people agree that being held accountable is good — yet so few allow themselves to actually be held accountable. If you or someone you care about would benefit from higher accountability, I want to offer a simple step that will allow more effective results. Here's the step, are you ready for it?

Be specific.

I told you it was simple! And while it may not be complex, it is astoundingly difficult in practice. If, for example one day you wake up and want to embark on a journey to get healthier (lose weight, feel better, exercise etc...) and all you do is state "I am going to get healthy!" there is almost no effective way to hold you to account. The statistical probability that you will actually accomplish your goal is very low as well, because you simply have not been specific. It would be much like asking an accountant to provide you a Profit and Loss Statement and the bottom line reads "you kinda made some profit." Or a Cash Flow Statement that says "you don't have much cash." You would fire that accountant immediately!

Accounting, just like accountability, is futile without specificity. It is very possible that your life and your business can soar to new heights if you will get specific. It may not be easy, but it will be fruitful.

Priority Management

The concept of Priority Management and ordering one's day for the most effective and fruitful result is a main focus of coaching. Too many of us have an idea of what we want our day to be when we get out of bed in the morning... then by 10:00 there have been enough distractions to disarm us for the remainder of the day! Five o'clock rolls around and we ask ourselves the ubiquitous question "Where did today go?" In a world where people are often screaming for your attention, keeping the commitments that you make to yourself is tricky business. We get trapped in the mire of putting aside the important to deal with the urgent. You may be shocked at how much of your life is dealing with something that is "urgent." The issue becomes acute — if not lethal — when you continue to pile more and more urgencies on.

Now, I must admit that I am dazzled at some people's propensity to manage their urgencies. But if so much of your business and life gets filled only by these urgencies, some obvious (and some not so obvious) things begin to happen. First the obvious: Stress! Health concerns and ineffectiveness can permeate your world.

The not-so-obvious is that so many of the things that you tell yourself are important get pushed to the back burner. At the very core of leading a disciplined life is doing the things that are important while decisively and courageously turning away from that which is urgent.

We mustn't keep piling on the urgency — there is a breaking point. You can justify the urgent until the cows come home, but you will still wake up and have to face this fact: there are disciplines, which are important, that you must execute if you are going to be fruitful. Don't live your life in a state of "Urgency Management." Stay true to what is important in your business and your life.

Hearty Work

There is an axiom in the business world that says "work smart, not hard." I get it, and I have even uttered the words myself. Yet there is something eerily wrong with this advice, as it can be interpreted in a way that may lead us into disaster. I would never coach someone to not work smart. We all need to delegate effectively, to ensure that we are doing what we do best, and to be vigilant with our time. All of this may fall under the category of "smart" work.

This could very well be the right time to re-evaluate what and to whom you are delegating. You may need to re-establish actions that keep you in your gifted zone or re-commit yourself to your daily disciplines.

But — and this is a big "but" — if you do all of those things and you miss the key of working hard, then you could be in for a disappointing season. Hard work is a crucial ingredient for almost every successful endeavor.

During each Olympic season, we have the opportunity to watch countless stories about what it takes to become successful. Each athlete's story has its own flavor and flair, but the common thread is that every one of these people had to put in their time. And so must we.

I cannot imagine a coach of one of these world class athletes asking their future gold medalist if they feel like working out or training in preparation for their big day. Every time the games roll around we watch in awe and wonder as these athletes skate, ski, or leap their way to a podium. It is almost magical to watch. And yet behind all of it, every one of these great athletes and coaches will tell you that the one unifying component of success is how hard the athlete worked.

I am all for working smart, but the success of the season that lies ahead of us will likely depend on our own willingness to work hard and smart. With our heads and our hearts.

Cutting Corners

It's amazing what you can learn on a run. Now, I know some of you learn while playing golf and others of you learn by reading books or listening to tapes… but I learn while running. The other day when I was running, I noticed a small patch of grass just off the sidewalk I was going to turn onto. If I took the grass, it would have shaved less than a second and a hardly measurable distance from my run. Still, I was tempted to cut the corner in the spirit of finishing my run just that much faster.

It struck me that we all have opportunities daily to cut corners. As the times get progressively tighter, it may get increasingly appealing to shave our standards just a bit — all for the sake of a little gain. My coaching on this is simple — don't do it.

Cutting little things here and there jeopardizes the biggest things we stand for. Let us all walk tall and do everything in our power to continue to take the proverbial high road. Even when a decision or an action seems small and innocuous, if making it is against your core principles, don't do it.

Every one of us has countless decisions daily where we could cut corners; most of them would scarcely ever even come to light. Still, the world will be a better place when even the small matters get our highest integrity. Stay off the grass.

Less Could Be More

What time are you leaving work today?

I once had a client ask me (in a somewhat disturbed tone) if I expected them to work until 10:00 PM. The question came on the heels of a discussion about disciplines that were committed to, but not adhered to because of a lack of time.

Neglecting our stated disciplines because we "don't have time" has got to be one of the most banal, monotonous things we hear as coaches. In this particular case, the frustrated individual concluded that the only possible way to get done what was needed was to simply tack more hours onto the day.

The truth is that you may accomplish more and become more disciplined by limiting your time rather than adding to it. I have tested this personally.

Around the same time, I received some positive feedback from another client who had made the decision to adhere to a rigid time block where he would not work past 5:30 — and on Fridays, he leaves at 4:00 sharp. By doing this, he successfully forced himself to be far more productive during the working hours. He is now doing more with his family and for his own health as a result.

The point is that sometimes, when we think strictly in terms of more hours, we unwittingly give ourselves permission to procrastinate or work in a way that is less than efficient.

Try it. It will not be easy at first, and you will likely feel some anguish as you leave at your own stated hour. But the pain that you feel will result in something even better for you in future days.

The limits you create are yours, but without limits you may continue to float in an endless sea of frustration, wondering how the days got away from you.

Get Back

We need to get back to the place we started from. It doesn't matter how seasoned you are — there are some basics that you did at the beginning of your career that were instrumental in getting you to where you are now. You made calls, wrote notes, knocked on doors, and executed on a series of activities that brought you success. Perhaps you did it to build momentum. Perhaps you did it out of necessity. Or, is it possible that you were just naïve enough to believe that these simple actions would yield results?

The key obstacle to getting back is your own ego. I have heard some say, "Oh no, I don't have to go make calls again, do I?" The answer of course is, "No, you don't." You are free to make any choice you want. But I beg you to consider making the choice to return to previous successes.

It may require a shift in your heart, but the good news is that it won't require a lot of training. You already know what it takes, because you've been down that road before.

Please do not minimize the potential impact of these actions. You may find it wonderfully refreshing. Or, you might catch yourself wondering if you still have what it takes to make it happen. The answer is YES, you do. But you can't know that unless you go back and do it.

So there you have it. Now it is your turn. What one or two simple steps brought you success? When will you get back?

Slipping

I once heard an adage that claimed, "In life there is no such thing as standing still; you are either moving forward or backward." Sometimes I have to admit that I wish this weren't accurate. It would be nice to coast for a while, to not have to constantly think of improving. But when you coast, most of the time you begin to slip back into old patterns and old behaviors. This is as true in the physical universe as it is in our businesses and our lives. When left alone, most things move to chaos and disorder — they do not improve by themselves. Thus, every day we must wake up and ask ourselves how we can be a little better. We must think how a little improvement may further us on our path, and we must look for those ways in which we have inadvertently slipped back. We all slip. The problem is that when we slip, sometimes we don't have the energy or fortitude to get back on the proverbial horse.

Perhaps you have fallen backwards multiple times and you just feel like giving up. Perhaps you are battle-worn and you simply don't feel like you have it in you to saddle up one more time. Actually, you do have it in you. But you may have to fight to get your mojo back.

The fight you must engage in is in your own heart and in your head. One question we coaches often get is "How do we keep this fight up?" While there is no one-size-fits-all answer, I can tell you that you may need to rediscover why you do what you do, where you are headed, and why it is important to stay on the path.

In the meantime, if you have felt the ubiquitous slip in a discipline or habit, one thing I highly recommend is to get back to the core of why it was important. When you get your WHY back, you will be back on the path.

Fight Disorganization

"Cleanliness is next to Godliness." I certainly hope there are other things next to Godliness. But when I ask my clients, "What one activity will help you in the most powerful way right now?" many simply reply, "Get organized." Stop right now, look around, and ask yourself if cleaning your desk and getting your world more organized would be helpful. While there are endless other activities that may seem more urgent, it has never ceased to amaze me how having order helps shape my overall world view.

I wouldn't dare claim to be the expert at keeping order, and I am grateful for the many people and systems that help me stay that way.

It is a good thing to keep recommitting to organization. It may be as simple as setting aside one hour after work or as complex as an entire Saturday, but committing the time to get organized is step one.

The next thing you want to do is declare a desired end result. What will a more organized workspace look like, and what will the implications be for your daily life? This is not new to any of us who have been through a vision exercise of any kind, but it is important to completing the task.

Finally, order and organization are not limited to what your desk and office look like. While they are great places to start, perhaps you need to clean up your e-mail in-box, update your family calendar, or de-clutter some other part of a system in your life. The fact is that when we are as compressed with the ways of life as we seem to be, orderliness can inadvertently take a back seat to productivity. But ironically, productivity suffers when orderliness disappears.

Discipline yourself to get back to order — you will be grateful you did.

Unsmothered

Over and over, I see my clients in a condition that can only be described as "smothered." They are so busy with activity that it is seemingly impossible to get it all done. What very few like to hear is that they are the ones that have created this condition. They make choices that pack their days full, and then they wonder how it got so packed.

If you attempt to accomplish important things in your business or your life, only to have your day "get away from you," the first step toward curing this problem is owning the fact that you let it get away.

In his book *First Things First*, Stephen Covey covered this quite accurately in his work on the Important/Urgent matrix. Too often, we give into urgency and then scratch our heads about why we aren't getting to more important things. There are some urgent things in life that require our attention, but if your day is filled with one urgent action after another, you may come to a point when the important things aren't getting accomplished.

A classic example of this is our physical health. Sadly, I see a lot of people who simply don't make their physical health a priority. Most of the time it is not urgent, but I think we can all agree that it is very important. It is amazing that we can put "working out" in our calendar, and then snooze that activity repeatedly because a client needs us now, or a business transaction must get moved forward, or a call comes in that takes us in another direction...

I only use exercise as one example. The truth is that there are many disciplines that we label as important to our lives and our success, and yet we choose urgency over and over again.

You can get unsmothered, but it will take courage: the courage to turn away from the incessant drip of urgency. This will require you to say 'no' from time to time. Try it. Do it with grace and professionalism.

Usually, those things you thought had to be done right now will still be there waiting after you take care of what is truly more important.

Lose the Snooze

How do we beat procrastination? To solve that problem would be to take a gigantic leap forward in the human race.

I honestly doubt that a simple paragraph could cure anyone of repeated procrastination, but I would like to propose that if you are one who procrastinates (don't we all suffer at some level) then perhaps you would consider a new course of action. We must have the courage to do something new. If not, then we are relegated to the ranks of people who give up and accept mediocre outcomes. Here's my proposal: if you are one who wakes up in the morning to an alarm clock, but you have a habit of snoozing the clock until it insists you get up, then starting tomorrow I would ask you to stop snoozing. Simply set your alarm for the time you want, and put your feet on the ground when your clock goes off. This may seem inane and possibly irrelevant, but consider this: the snooze button on your alarm clock is much like the snooze button in your business and in your life.

We often go to great lengths to create systems and structures to help us with the activities that we know we should do. I have coached people who have created very elaborate systems all designed to help them just get it done. Then, when the alarm goes off... we snooze it. Our freedom to choose to snooze our activities is very powerful and very destructive. If you are caught in a pattern of habitually snoozing your stated disciplines, I call upon you to lose the snooze. Start in the morning. Let the first thing you do in your day be indicative of how you will conduct yourself throughout the day. You will be stunned at just what you can do if you simply stop snoozing.

The Courage to Measure

Frequently, I speak with people who want to understand how they can take their desired actions to completion. There are as many ideas about this as there are questions. One proven way you can help yourself is to measure your activity and your results. This advice sounds so over-simplified that often people ignore it. The truth is that by measuring, we also keep the stated discipline at the top of our mind. By raising our awareness, we raise our effectiveness. I have rarely come across an individual who doesn't understand the correlation between measurement and results. And yet, such a gap still exists. Why?

We could spend an eternity trying to understand why we don't measure when we know we should, but in the end that would just be one more means of deflection. So I will offer just one possibility, because sometimes by naming the enemy we can beat the enemy. Measuring is tedious. It offers no sense of thrill whatsoever. Frankly, it is a bit boring. Ironically, the result of measuring is quite the opposite. Consider what it feels like to take something to completion, to know your hard work paid off with a win. The moment of achievement is exhilarating.

We need to accept the fact that most of the activities on the road to victory offer no euphoric sense at all. Measuring is a good 'ol fashioned boring discipline, and the people who do it effectively will reap the benefit. Anyone can say that they are going to go win. Few make the time to put a tangible action into place, and fewer still find the courage to measure. You could be one of those few.

My hope is that, as you make commitments to take needed actions in your life and business, you will also make the choice to measure them. No one can promise it will be any fun, but it will bring you closer to the goal. Let's get crackin'!

The Heavier Weight

Jim Rohn once said, "We all must suffer one of two things: the pain of discipline or the pain of regret or disappointment."

Jim claims that both a disappointed life and a disciplined life are painful. But one is far more painful than the other, and you don't have to think too hard to guess which one. I appreciate the reality behind the idea that leading a disciplined life is not a cake walk. All too often we form the expectation that life should be easy.

Make no mistake, creating disciplines means creating boundaries, and boundaries (even those we put on ourselves) are painful. But isn't it fascinating that if we submit ourselves to this kind of pain, we usually get more of the thing we were shooting for? Never let anyone convince you that being disciplined is easy or free of pain. The truth is that it is difficult and will always require something from you. The discipline of exercise, for example, is painful for most. But the result of failing to exercise is much weightier (no pun intended) and far more devastating over time. This is not a particularly new insight, and yet so many people continue to have businesses and lives that exchange the weight of discipline for the much heavier weight of an undisciplined life.

We would all do well to submit ourselves to the pain of discipline. Where in your life or in your business does this apply? I began with a Jim Rohn quote, and now I will end with one: "Success is nothing more than a few simple disciplines practiced every day." Make today great.

Law School

There are many laws that we must abide by in life. There are laws that we create as humans, and there are ones that simply exist in the Universe. We would be wise to buckle our seatbelts, and we would be foolish to try and thwart the law of gravity. Not too long ago, a few thought leaders and authors picked up on the idea that there are laws in business and life. We have now spun off many a book about "the law of this" and "the law of that."

One law that seems to be amazingly accurate is what Jim Rohn called the "Law of Diminishing Intent." We often attend seminars or read books and end by claiming, "I will go and do this!" Then life happens and we don't.

This is all too common, which is why it is so powerful to understand the Law of Diminishing Intent. I often bring it up when I conduct a seminar because it is my hope that I can help people avoid it.

It recently struck me that the law, while very real, is also somewhat negative. Our intentions do indeed diminish over time. But focusing only on that is like playing golf when there is a lake in front of you, and you repeat to yourself "don't hit the lake, don't hit the lake, don't hit the lake..." Where do you think that ball is going?

The good players never think "don't hit the lake." They only think "hit the grass." It may seem trivial, but what you say to yourself in your own head ends up being enormously important. Today, I propose a new law to supplement the Law of Diminishing Intent. I shall hereby call it the "Law of Promising Choice."

After all, you do have a choice. You do not need to fall victim to diminished intentions. It seems to make much more sense to focus on what you can do rather than on the possibility of failure. We will hit much more grass if we guide our thoughts to what is possible.

Sensefullness

I have always marveled at bumper stickers. I don't really understand why people want to advertise their thoughts on their cars. Some are funny, I suppose, but many are just odd. One such bumper sticker reads, "Practice random acts of kindness and senseless acts of beauty." I understand the intended meaning. But in practice, why would you want any action — especially a good, productive one — to be random?

My clients often admit to me that there are actions they know they should be taking, but they just aren't happening. For example, I coach some leaders who know that they should catch people doing things right and praise them for it. However, to praise someone genuinely is a matter of the heart, and it should just happen... randomly.

If there is a spontaneous action you know you should be doing, I do not see anything wrong with actually sticking it in your calendar. If the discipline has to do with something personal, and you aren't remembering to do it, then actually writing it down is certainly permissible.

I have people reminding themselves to call family and friends, to get up and visit with people in their office, to wish their loved ones a happy birthday or happy anniversary. Now, you may want to write it in a way that only you understand — something cryptic that causes a memory trigger for you.

I know at first this may seem contrived, and certainly you need to get to a point where the action is happening spontaneously. But in the meantime, some of the things we need to do must find their way to our calendars so that we can ensure that they get done. This is why the randomness of acts of kindness is such a poor idea. The truth is that, when we allow our actions to be random, often the action doesn't happen at all. It was Jim Collins who said that "The signature of mediocrity is chronic inconsistency."

Let us not be mediocre with our actions. Plug them into your calendar, even if it feels weird. Eventually they will become habits.

Back to High Ground

In 1984, legendary downhill skier Phil Mahre won a gold medal in the Olympics in what was then called Yugoslavia. Many of you may remember Phil's feat as he edged out his twin brother, Steve, to take home the gold. A few years ago, I was fortunate to be able to interview Phil in front of a group in Lake Tahoe. It was amazing to listen to Phil as his emotions ran high about an event that happened so many years ago. Phil brought an amazing amount of wisdom as he spoke about the courage and work ethic it took to make it to the podium and hear our National Anthem.

One component of his talk had to do with slumps. He told us that every great athlete has them, and by translation we all assumed that every great leader and business person has them, too. The simple fact is, slumps happen. But it is Phil's remedy for a slump that I feel compelled to share with you. I believe that if we can embrace this then any one of us can escape a slump and be back on the high road of positive momentum and forward progress.

Here's the cure: go back to basics.

That's it. It may not be sexy, and you may want to believe that it is something far more dynamic and convoluted. The truth is that every great athlete, artist, leader, or salesperson has fundamentals that can be re-examined and re-mastered. You may be in a slump right now. You may be coming out of one, or there may be one lying in wait just around the corner. It isn't a matter of "if" but "when."

Remember that the fundamentals of your job can and will pull you out of a slump. It may be as simple as asking yourself, "What did I first do to have success in my current role?" Get back to that, and you will be stunned at how quickly you can rebound.

Thank God I Was Doing That!

Let's play a little game.

Close your eyes and consider for a moment what you think will happen in the year ahead. Where do you think the economy will be? What direction do you think your company will go? Do you predict steady growth? Do you see good things or bad? Now, imagine that the second half of the year will be rough. Sales slow down considerably, and all around things are bleak. Imagining that you really did have a brutal second half of the year, what do you suppose would make you look back and exclaim, "Thank God I was doing that!"

Can you identify exactly what "that" would be? Is it a specific strategy, a discipline, or a project? If you can figure out your "that," you may uncover the very discipline you need to master right now. For the record, I don't think that these kinds of head games should be played often. You can always find someone who is predicting more challenging times ahead, and it isn't good for us to live in negativity. It is poison to the soul. The point of this little game is to help uncover the activity that you should be doing anyway. And if no such tough times come to pass, the only downside for you is that you will have been living a more disciplined life — something which will serve you well no matter what the year brings. As a good friend of mine says, "Live Ready!"

Unseen Reward

It is not uncommon for me to assign action plans that lead my clients into daily routines that may seem mundane, repetitive, boring, or small. Outbound calls, handwritten notes, and simple gestures make your business go forward. Jim Rohn once said, "Success is neither magical nor mysterious. Success is the natural consequence of consistently applying the basic fundamentals."

I have observed something mysterious that occurs when you apply the basic fundamentals in business or in life. Sometimes, you get results in other arenas. It is almost as if you are being rewarded for your discipline, but the reward arrives from a seemingly unrelated source.

Have you ever wondered why you engage for the good… and then stop? Perhaps it is because we don't interpret our efforts correctly. We don't see the correlation between the activity that we are doing and the positive results that we are getting, so we give up on the activity too quickly.

Let's say that you are committed to the fundamental of making daily outbound calls to past clients. I'd be shocked if you told me that for every call you made, you got a sale. (If it were that easy, everyone would do it.) Instead, I'd expect to hear that the calls are going ok, and maybe you're not so sure whether you see the benefit.

But as you repeat the action, other positive things begin to occur in your business. Perhaps a call you made three weeks ago yields unexpected results today. It could be that pushing yourself to follow through with this discipline increases your follow-through with other disciplines. Your positive momentum can further improve the way you interact with your team, or plan for next year, or connect with a referral partner…

Activity breeds activity, but not always in the way we expect. Thus, if the benefit is indirect and we don't interpret it well, then we may stop doing the activity — only to wonder what happened to our other successes. Make up your mind to engage in the fundamentals. Measuring has great merit, but don't forget that there may be some unintended reward that your measurements can't capture.

THE VALUE OF RELATIONSHIPS

May you find victory and strength in numbers.

No Neutral Encounters

There are no neutral encounters. Anytime you meet someone — whether it be over the phone, at the check-out counter of your local grocery store, or during a deep personal conversation on a 4-hour flight — the two parties will leave each other a little better or a little worse. There is no neutrality.

You may fight this idea, or simply take for granted that brief encounters may be neutral. The truth is that what you say, how you say it, how you smile (or don't), your body language and tone of voice all lead to a general impression which impacts each person in either a positive or negative way.

If you believe this, then think of how it could challenge you and make you think differently about your business and your life.

Imagine the ramifications in your relationships if you realized that you had such an impact. How would you respond differently if you were aware of what was at stake in each personal encounter?

I do not believe that you could always leave everyone better — we are human after all. But I do believe that simple awareness of this fact could change the way you approach and speak to people, and create a more positive impression in even the briefest of interactions.

What may this world look like if more people knew they could leave so many better?

Give Your Best to Your Best

I am not 100% certain where I first heard this idiom. Like many concepts that come out through the coaching process, a saying like this one can take on a meaning that is different from its original intent. In the realm of your personal life, giving your best often applies to your family.

Daniel Harkavy, CEO of Building Champions, shared this with me a few years back as I was lamenting how often I came home after a day at work and was essentially drained and needing to have a bit of selfish "couch time" to recover before engaging with my family. The truth is, that was a mistake and it was a clear example of not giving my best to my best — they often got the leftovers of my day. How unfair.

For a few months I kept a Post-It® note on my dashboard that simply read "GYBTYB." That note reminded me that, when I entered my home after being at work, I needed to be ready to give my heart and my time to the very people I consider to be my best. That ridiculous Post-It® would often cause me to pull over on the side of the road to contemplate the day and compose myself.

The GYBTYB concept applies at work, too. Your best may be the people that support you, or even your colleagues. Giving these people your seconds leads to a support system that cannot sustain a good level of service. GYBTYB also applies to your customers. It is likely that there are a few people in your world who are very dedicated and loyal to you. I want to encourage you to treat these people with special care and give them your very best.

I know that there will be some who will assume that this means giving others your worst. By all means, you should treat every customer with dignity and respect. There are a select few, however, who have been dedicated to your success. It makes great business sense to give of your first fruits to those individuals.

Try it. I believe you will see the results.

Connection

"The mass of men lead lives of quiet desperation." This is one of Henry David Thoreau's more somber quotes. What a horribly negative, cynical thing to say about mankind. There are vast possibilities for the reason we would lead such bleak lives, but the most common is that people have a tendency to isolate themselves.

As we age, many of us have an increasingly difficult time connecting with other people. You would be blown away to learn just how many people around you have no deep friendships or close connections.

I guess it is safer that way. Without intimacy and closeness, no one can hurt you — right? Perhaps. But in the end, we were made to be in communities and relationships.

We live in this bizarre, individualistic culture that strangely promotes aloneness. Now, I am all for a little quiet, meditative time, but most of us actually need to reach out and stay connected to friends, family, and colleagues. Staying connected to people brings with it a level of accountability that can be healthy. I am not sure I have ever met a serious individual who wouldn't admit that accountability is a good thing. But when we isolate, we further increase our propensity to think and act in ways that are incongruent with our own values.

It is certainly possible to be over-connected and allow too much and too many in your life as well. But if I were a betting man, I would say that the much greater need is to connect more, not less. Reach out to someone today. It may not be the safest move you make, but at least you will be taking steps to not be a part of Thoreau's masses.

Never Doubt

I don't really have a favorite quote. I am, however a huge fan of some people's ability to put concise, thought-provoking ideas into words. When gifted artists put these words to music, the lyrics can be magical. Van Morrison, Paul Simon, and Jackson Browne are living examples of singer-songwriters who have an uncanny ability with words. Perhaps you have a favorite musician yourself. There are also authors and teachers like Jim Rohn, Zig Ziglar and John Maxwell who have such a talent with words.

One quote that has struck me frequently is by Margaret Mead. She said, "Never doubt that a small group of dedicated people can change the world; indeed it is the only thing that ever has." A small group of dedicated people. I have been with such a group, and the power generated from a gathering of like-minded people is remarkable.

We need to keep coming together in groups. That group may be as small as a handful of people or as large as a roomful, but if we are to change the world we must realize that we are much more likely to do so in packs. And yet, we find it so easy to isolate.

The other side of Mead's quote about changing the world is Thoreau's quote about how most men lead lives of "quiet desperation." Who could possibly change the world in such circumstances? The good news is that you don't have to try. What you must do is continue to pursue your pack, your posse, the people you run with.

Find a group that will lift you up and encourage your goals and dreams. Find people who love you enough to speak the truth to you. Do this, and you will find yourself in the best possible situation. Stay connected. The world needs you, and you will have more to give to the world when you are part of such a great network.

Trust

Are you a person that trusts others? Do people trust you? These are broad questions that surely don't have a one dimensional answer.

Developing trust seems to be at the epicenter of a good relationship. When you have a solid business relationship with someone, it is often one where both parties have developed trust with one another over some period of time. And yet, it is such an ethereal, esoteric concept. How do we go about intentionally building trust with others?

If you want to expand your professional relationships — the kind that are built on trust and result in good reciprocating business — I recommend that you start by becoming more trusting of others. Now, we live in a fallen, broken and dark world. You will be given ample reasons not to trust people throughout your life. In fact, it is highly likely that you can stop right now and come up with hundreds of reasons not to trust, based on empirical evidence of bad circumstances in your life when you did trust someone. My coaching to you today is to trust anyway. Even in the face of having been burned before. I am not implying that you should be gullible and lack discernment. I have simply observed that many who want to increase their business as a result of building higher trust with people need to start by trusting others more readily.

Counter Intuition

We have all heard of counterintelligence. The FBI and other organizations in the US and abroad employ such agencies "thwarting the efforts of an enemy's intelligence agents to gather information or commit sabotage". Lately, I have found a need to share with many clients a plan for "counter intuition." I doubt anyone will go off and form a government agency over it, but counter intuition comes into play frequently in business and in life.

A perfect example of using counter intuition is in the realm of trust. This can be so "intuitive" when we get burned by someone or something that we develop an aversion to whatever or whoever burned us.

If we get burned repeatedly and in succession it is quite intuitive to create a posture of cynicism and to become skeptical. Difficult times can cause even the brightest people to become dull as they acquiesce to the situations that repeatedly get them down.

I say you should never let anyone or any situation ever get you to the point where your soul becomes jaded, even at the risk of being slightly vulnerable. Because when we do become jaded, we lose much more than what the situation warranted — we lose the pieces of us that make us attractive to others.

It is so intuitive to react this way and easy to justify why you are down and guarded. This is why we need counter intuition. Fight back! Do not carry burdens or anger. When we allow our own hearts to become jaded, we may lose something bigger than we ever thought possible. Don't let it happen.

Trust is a great thing… even when your intuition tells you not to.

Your Competitive Essence

When we lead people or sell things to people there are two essential components of the interaction: one is technical and the other is personal. The technical side, called Form, is all about the tangible, empirical aspects of what you bring to the table. It's the product you are selling and the system you use to sell it.

How many books and seminars have we invested in over the years to learn how to become product experts and masters of the technical components of our vocations? I will not dispute the validity of this. It is important.

On the other hand, there is a side to our interactions that is far less tangible and virtually immeasurable. It is the relational component, and it is equally vital to our success. We shall refer to this as Essence.

The mastery of both Form and Essence is crucial. Interestingly, the world we live in will tell you that Form is what really matters. Because Essence is so intangible, it is often discarded as fluffy, feel-good malarkey. Thus, more and more people get trapped into thinking they can distinguish themselves through better and better Form. It is important to know your product well and to be technically excellent at your job, but you may find that many people will do business with you simply because they like you and trust you. "Likeability" and "trust" are but two examples of Essence.

Somebody out there can and will outperform you in the category of Form. They will have a better product, a better rate, and a better system. But if you master Essence, you may find yourself standing alone atop the podium. The bottom line is that both Form and Essence are important, but Essence is where you will have your greatest opportunity to distinguish yourself.

Relationship Creation

It doesn't matter how long you have been in your current role, how educated you are, or where you happen to be in the current cycle of your business. We all need relationships in our businesses if we are to be successful. The question that I hear over and over again is, "How do I create new business relationships?"

I want to offer a simple approach to creating new relationships, and I am going to express it first as an equation. It goes like this:

New Relationships = Time + Intentionality + A North-Facing Compass

Let me break that down a little further:

Time. We must understand that any lasting business relationship (or personal one, for that matter) comes as a result of time spent with that individual. Do you have the time blocked on your calendar?

Intentionality. We must make our efforts intentional. Relationships rarely emerge or deepen by accident, and they won't magically appear just because we sit around and dream that they will.

True North. This one is a bit more difficult, because it has to do with our hearts. We can create the time and be intentional, but if our primary motivation in creating this relationship is to get business and make money, then our efforts will ultimately fail. Technically, you can lie about your intentions, but eventually the truth will come out. The best thing you can do is to question your own motives for wanting the relationship. Remember, we are speaking about a new relationship. If the recipient of your time and intentionality learned that your core motive was to make money, how incentivized would they be to invest their time in you?

This is a simple strategy, but it could cause some of us to do some intensive heart surgery before we go out and seek the company of others again.

The ironic twist is that, if your heart is right, the time + intentionality piece becomes much easier.

Beyond "Customer" Service

I'm always fascinated when I hear terms like "relationship selling." It makes me wonder — is there any other kind of selling? I realize that we do sell programs and products, gadgets and intellectual property. So much of sales, however, comes down to the relationships we establish with one another.

A commonly overlooked principle of excellent customer service is providing service to everyone, not just your customers. Why not create a plan to make sure you are looking out for your vendors and those who sell to you? Unfortunately, it is all too common to treat vendors and service providers like second-class citizens. None of us like to be offered that kind of treatment, so why would it be a part of the way we do business? Instead, treat them just like you would if they were your key clients. This is one more way to banish an entitlement mindset that can lead to scarcity thinking. John Maxwell wrote a book entitled *There's No Such Thing as "Business" Ethics.* Maxwell makes the point that there are only "ethics," and if you don't have them in life then you won't have them in business.

Customer service is the same way. Perhaps someone needs to write a book called *There's No Such Thing as "Customer" Service.* There is only "service." If you don't have a conviction in your heart about serving all people, then you'll never be excellent at serving your customers. Couldn't we all get a little better at that? I know I can.

Groups, Tribes and Posses

I once started a running group. It was quite simple, really. We sent out an e-mail inviting about 10 people to show up for a run.

"Our group will meet at noon twice a week at the building across the street, and we will run." Why on earth would you care? Actually, I assume you don't care at all about our little group of wanna-be health nuts, but what you may care about is how you can put together a group of your own.

I am continually surprised by the persistence of the gravitational pull away from communities. Our lives are so busy that it's easy to create an excuse for not meeting with people. Let's face it, people are a pain. Relationships are a pain. So we convince ourselves that life would be simpler if we could all just be left alone.

One of my mentors once told me that every fear of the human heart can be traced back to the fear of being left alone. If you were ever left alone as a child, you know exactly what I am talking about. How strange, then, that we have this tendency to isolate.

I say let's come against that tendency and create groups, tribes, posses and gatherings of all kinds. Engage! Yes, there will be pain, disappointment, frustration, and conflict. But there will also be laughter, support, encouragement, and camaraderie. And make no mistake — aloneness is infinitely and eternally worse.

Go join a club — or create one — where you share some common interest and encourage those around you to do the same. There is an enemy in the world that we cannot see, and he would love to see us all alone. May your engagement be a direct assault on his plan. May you find victory and strength in numbers.

... And In the End

I have to assume it is common knowledge that relationships are the foundation of a healthy business. In fact, relationships are the foundation of a healthy life. Has anyone ever found in human history an example of a healthy, happy person going through life alone?

And yet, as obviously critical as they may be, we all still struggle with relationships. Ironically, the closest relationships seem to be the hardest to maintain. Your family and friends are often the source of the deepest contention in your life. Isn't that amazing? The fact that we all want relationships, and yet we have to fight so hard to sustain or grow them, is ample evidence that there is something in the universe set against us.

Folks, there is an enemy. "Divide and Conquer" has got to be one of his craftiest tools. If you doubt this, consider the divorce rate in our country these days.

The people who will become the most successful in life and in business will be those who have the most impenetrable relationships. In the end, it's what it will all be about.

The stunning truth about relationships is that you have great control over how many you have and how deep they are. If we can put down our pride, forgive freely, and care genuinely about the well-being of others, we will experience a richer life. Something so simple, and still so rare. I propose that we all make it more commonplace. Let us all do this better and usher in a new generation of success.

In the end, the equation is quite simple. Better relationships = better life, better business, better everything. The enemy be damned!

EFFECTIVE COMMUNICATION

You have an extraordinary ability to make someone's life better through the power of your words.

Get Smart

There may never be a better time and place to work on your Emotional Intelligence than right here and now. Let me offer a simple definition of Emotional Intelligence: it is our ability to respond to circumstances in a way that is congruent with our beliefs. Someone who exhibits high Emotional Intelligence can find themselves in a situation that would cause most people to snap, send an awful e-mail, or generally freak out. But because this individual has great awareness of how they are feeling, they are able to quickly assess the situation and control how they respond.

Think about it. Haven't there been situations that have caused you to react in a way that you later regretted because your behavior was not in line with what you see as the most appropriate response? There seem to be an infinite number of situations hitting us these days which require us to deploy high Emotional Intelligence in order to obtain the success we desire. Economic hardships, relational strain, corporate and governmental policies and a myriad of other circumstances are hammering at us. One of the great ways to weather these storms is to be thoughtful about your EQ.

It is said that there are three components that comprise who we are: 1) our past experiences, 2) our IQ (which is our capacity to learn, not how "smart" we are), and 3) our Emotional Quotient (or EQ), the measure of our Emotional Intelligence. Of these three, the only one you can change is your EQ.

It may seem like a blinding flash of the obvious, but there is little or nothing we can do to change the circumstances around us. Fortunately, there is much we can do to change our response to them. Study after study shows that the most fruitful and successful people in life are not necessarily the smartest, but rather those who gain control of their responses to any given environment.

I leave you with a biblical quote: "Do not conform to the pattern of this world, but be transformed by the renewing of your mind." (Romans 12:2) A little "mind renewing" could do us all some good.

Louder Than Words

There is a timeless axiom that says "actions speak louder than words." Just about everyone has heard this saying, and yet ironically these words often don't have much impact. It could be one of the highest forms of Emotional Intelligence to understand that you are saying something with every one of your actions.

Whether we are speaking to a large group or having a critical one-on-one conversation, we ponder and practice what we are going to say. Our words can certainly have an amazing impact on people. It is wise to choose good words, because we can build someone up or tear them down in an instant with our words.

Do we ever stop to consider that we can do the same thing with our actions?

If our actions speak louder than our words, then we have an even greater capacity to grow something great or destroy it with incredible force. Our actions carry an immense responsibility. Remember that inaction is also a kind of action. If you choose not to do anything today, you may miss an opportunity to build a great thing. I have coached many people who struggle with inaction. They may not realize it, but their inaction speaks louder than their words.

Inaction says that you are unwilling to put yourself out there. Inaction speaks of a lack of courage. When you hold back on doing something you know could build up others, you are sending the message that those others are not worth the risk. I implore you to take that risk. When your actions have the intent to help and care for others, then the likelihood of going astray is greatly diminished.

Make that call. Write that note. See that person. Say something powerful with your actions!

A Force to be Reckoned With

It is stunning just how fast that field of "social media" has grown. Blogging, Myspace, Facebook, LinkedIn®, Twitter... they have gone from 0 to 100 MPH, faster than any car ever claimed. In fact, by the time these words are in print, half of what I am about to say could be outdated.

I am overwhelmed by the idea of writing on this topic, because I'm not sure how to approach it in a way that hasn't been already covered by millions of others. Social media is an indisputably amazing technological phenomenon, and there are countless ways in which these tools can serve you.

In this world of instant communication, we have an unparalleled ability to help others through our words and pictures... but we also have greater capacity to do instant harm and lasting damage. In the field of Emotional Intelligence there are two components of self awareness: an individual component and a social component. Social awareness teaches us to be conscious of what we do and say in the world around us.

When you are on Facebook, for example, it is good practice to re-read everything before you post. Be aware that entire networks of people are reading it, and it is going to be assimilated in a way that is personal to them. A stunning number of people commit social media suicide because they are not as aware as they should be when they post thoughts, ideas, and plans out there for all to see.

For the record, I am a fan of these tools. But unlike any other communication mechanism in our history, they have an immediate ability to harm you and others if you are not careful about what you put out there. May we all grow in our social awareness as we grow in the world of social media. Be discerning about how you say what you say, and be thoughtful about where you say it. You never know into whose eyes and ears your message will fall.

These tools are an amazing force. Please use the force wisely.

Think. Act. In That Order

In substance abuse recovery, there is a commonly used acronym — HALT — which has an application in many areas of life, including stress management and decision making. Never make key life decisions when you are Hungry, Angry, Lonely or Tired.

In today's fast-paced, frenetic world, many people are coming to key conclusions under stress. The decisions that they make under these conditions are far from the ones that will serve them best. For many of us, this is a high-pressure time, and emotions are swinging wildly. For some, business is really great. For others, it is simply very difficult. Either way, the environment is such that we are frequently in that zone in which making reckless key decisions could be disastrous.

There is a wonderful Proverb that states "all a man's ways seem right to him…" (Romans 21:2) In a high-stress moment, it could seem completely justifiable to make a snap decision. But the truth is that, if we would only remember to pause and step back in those moments, we could all save ourselves from some unintended consequences.

This whole concept is the very essence of Emotional Intelligence. Let's all remember to step back and allow time to shed light on reason. If we would all collectively make that commitment, our decisions would have their best chance at serving our futures.

Cheers to high self-awareness and not allowing high-flying emotions to take over your actions.

Fakebook

Recently, a client of mine pointed out that very few people ever put anything controversial on Facebook. Who tweets about their struggles or blogs about the real pain in their life?

Joe Smith is battling a drug addiction and it's threatening to tear my marriage apart.

Mary Jones is worried that, if we don't make some drastic changes, we're going to lose the house.

Adam Johnson is angry at God right now.

As a coach, I help people battle reluctance and fear daily. Good things do happen, but it's equally true that tough, painful things are a real part of life. We live in a world where it is still taboo to point them out. Thus, many people continue to pose in a way that covers over their deep struggles.

If you want to encourage people and bring joy into their lives, consider for a minute that you can often do that just by being real.

Many people don't want to show their pain and conflict to the world. So they hide. They cover over the ugly parts. Then, their shame is exacerbated when everyone else around them is pointing out how good everything is. I hope this isn't a big newsflash, but let me assure you that no one is happy, joy-filled, and content all of the time. All people struggle.

All people have doubts and fears. If you wrap your mind and heart around that, you may find it easier to go out and influence the world.

You needn't wait until you feel as good as the rest of the world appears to feel. You'll never compete with the posers, anyway. My friend called Facebook a twisted Wizard of Oz world. Consider all of the fake things in that world of Dorothy's — the singing munchkins and the horse of a different color laughing the day away in the merry old Land of Oz. But with all of the poppy fields and flying monkeys... even that world had pain and conflict.

Go help the world around you, even if you don't feel like bursting into song. In the end, even Dorothy preferred her real life over a beautiful fairy tale. You may learn that you can do even greater things in the reality of your very weakness.

Which and How

Sometimes it feels like life is a series of daily battles that we must face. That may sound a bit hostile, but from my coaches' chair I could tell story after story of the battles people face in their work and in their lives. I want to offer two simple thoughts about the nature of battles that we will inevitably face.

The first is 'WHICH.' There are some battles we should fight, and some we shouldn't. Discerning between these two could be a matter of saving your job or a key relationship.

There are times when we choose to stand and fight and, even if we win, we lose. The time and emotional energy required simply wasn't worth it. Some battles, as right as they may feel, are not worth the emotional, mental, or physical toll. Acquiescence and acceptance may be a better play.

The second is 'HOW.'

If you choose to stand and battle for what is right, then how you fight — the manner in which you choose your words, your tone, and your method of delivery — is crucial to your success. In the history of Major League Baseball, have you ever seen an umpire overturn a decision because some dirt-kicking, f-bomb throwing manager raced out to home plate to prove a point? Or is it possible that the only thing that was ever accomplished by them throwing their weight around was a trip to the locker room and a smaller strike zone from the angry ump? How you choose to say what you choose to say matters immensely. Let's keep our Emotional Intelligence high as we navigate through the storms of change.

The WHICH and HOW may carry some amazing saving grace for you. It is my hope that you consider how this applies to your world.

The One-Way Street of Social Media

When I was young, I assumed that by this time the earth would look more like the world of *The Jetsons*. Now that I think about it, maybe we're not far off. Facebook, blogging, Smartphones, Tweets... these previously unknown phenomena have become commonplace in our culture. These are the means by which we now communicate. As these methods of communication continue to evolve, I have noticed one enormous problem: few people really listen.

These technologies enable people to get their thoughts and ideas out there rapidly. But it's harder to demonstrate that you are really listening, that you understand what is being offered, and acknowledge the person behind the communication. Thus, much of Social Media is a one-way street.

Now, certainly you can reply or leave a comment and tell someone that you heard what they said and you are considering their thoughts and words. But even in responses, it often feels like another chance for others to push their own ideas on the subject. I believe that Social Media is still wonderful... as long as it encourages us to have real-life, face-to-face, in-person contact. It is only with this kind of contact that we can build authentic relationships.

I am not urging for the demise of all Social Media. But as our culture goes deeper and deeper into these forms of communication, my hope is that we will not leave behind authentic relationships. The kind where we can resolve conflict effectively through sincere listening and genuine presence with other human beings.

If our usage of Social Media connects us with real people and encourages us to be more in their physical presence, then we will win. With all of the acronyms that exist in this modern communication — like LOL — I propose a new one. HUC: Heard, Understood, Considering. It will never replace being in front of someone, but at least it's a start!

Giving Away What We Possess

My coach, Jack, calls them "green words." These are thoughts and ideas given away to others that are not yet fully developed in the speaker's own life. Much like unripe green fruit — they are "green words." This has convicted me to go back to my own writing and coaching and ask myself if I am simply trying to give away thoughts, ideas, and actions before I have experienced them myself. I challenge you to ask yourself the same question — "Am I experiencing in my life or business the very things I'm trying to convince the people around me to experience?"

With this thought, I have reviewed my own words and have challenged myself: Am I organized? Do I have unsubstantiated fears? Am I doing something about the "shoulds" in my own life and business? Have I dedicated time lately to thinking about the bigger "why" of my own life and business?

I cannot in good faith answer that I take all of my own medicine. But I realize that I need to drink more deeply from my own words, and I challenge you to do the same. There is a saying that "You cannot give away what you don't possess." I disagree entirely! When we use green words we are essentially trying to give away the things we do not yet possess. Perhaps this famous idiom could more accurately state that "We SHOULDN'T try and give away what we don't possess."

I am on a mission. Would you join me? What words, thoughts, or actions do you pass along to others that you need to drink deeper of yourself? We all need fewer green words.

Inviting with Your Voice

When you pick up the phone and say hello to someone — whether it is your home phone, cell, or work — remember that your first words and the tone they carry have an amazing ability to either invite or reject the caller. Answering our phones is so common that I think we have forgotten just how powerfully we can influence someone with our voice. It is one of those daily activities, done so frequently and unconsciously, that many of us underestimate its power.

How many times have you called a place of business looking for information, only to get someone on the other end that seemed almost bothered by your call? Chances are, the person answering is not actually bothered by the call, but the monotony of the activity can cause people to unconsciously lose the power their voice carries.

The good news is that there is ample room for us to get it right, and it takes so little effort. Try it.

Today, every time you pick up the phone, regardless of who it is on the other end, concentrate on making your tone and your words inviting. You will be surprised by the effect. You needn't take a course on the topic or even practice all of the perfect words. You simply need to understand that the person calling is going to quickly and unwittingly make a judgment about you, your business and your willingness based upon a few simple words. And you needn't sound like an enthusiastic game show host either, but rather someone who has the power to guide someone into feeling welcomed or rejected.

Every single one of us can do this a little better today. Make it great! And don't forget that there is no neutrality with relationships — you are either going to leave someone a little better or a little worse. Choose the prior!

The Power of Words

Never underestimate the power of your words. Our ability to make a difference in the lives of others with our words is remarkable. I think most of us would agree that somewhere in our lives, someone has said something to us which left an indelible mark on us. I am amazed at how some of the simplest and smallest of words can create such a lasting difference. It can be as small as a passing comment or as big as a well-thought-out personal letter or speech. Either way I want to invite you to consider how you have the ability to make such a difference with your words. You needn't be a great author or orator. Simply telling someone that they did well or that you are thinking of them can turn a dark day, bright.

Words like "I was thinking about what you said..." and "You make a difference!" and "Will you forgive me?" can change someone's world. Words can tear people down as well, but for now I want to remind you that you have an extraordinary ability to make someone's life better through your words. It is very easy to forget this fact. We inadvertently undervalue the power that we possess.

Perhaps there are times when we think that a note or a comment would be a bother or a distraction for someone and we miss an opportunity. There isn't a scenario I can think of whereby a kind note or encouragement from you would be a bother to someone. The continued commitment to the habit of using small words to encourage people in a big way can revolutionize your business and your life.

CARE AUTHENTICALLY

Consider what would change in your world (and in your pursuit of success) if you were to sincerely put your focus on the betterment of others.

Have Your Pie and Eat It, Too

Action, discipline, performance, and tenacity are some of the key traits that are foundational to success in business. Consider all of the books, tapes, seminars, and articles out there about how successful people adhere to the highest standards of action-oriented characteristics.

Fewer deal with the issue of likeability and authentic care for others. It is so easy to dismiss the idea of caring about others as feel-good hogwash. It may be that we need a refresher course on this topic because our narcissistic culture simply won't have us look in the mirror and ask how we can become kinder, more caring people.

There is a quote by Zig Ziglar that goes like this: "You can have everything in life you want if you will just help enough other people get what they want." It is a good and clever saying to be sure. But if you hear it wrong, the emphasis is still on what YOU get. Certainly the intent is to focus on helping others, but it fascinates me that we can still interpret it in a selfish way.

How about this: Help others get what they want, with little regard for your own gain.

I implore us all to take a few minutes to consider what would change in our worlds (and in our pursuit of success) if we were to sincerely put our focus on the betterment of others. I know there will be many who will brush this aside because the action it requires to look into such a mirror is too difficult. That's ok. But if you ever get to a point in your career or life when all of your strivings seem to be getting you nowhere, you might consider authentic care for people as a strategy. No one will promise you millions if you do, but you may find that this path leads to deeper more fulfilling relationships. It's funny: isn't this what we were shooting for with all of those actions all along?

Or is all of this just pie in the sky?

A More Lofty Pursuit

When our country formally declared independence, there was a document drafted and presented to the people of our country that still impacts us deeply all these years later. Today, one can scarcely make it out of the second grade without being able to recite the "unalienable rights" of Life, Liberty and the Pursuit of Happiness.

I'm not quite sure what it is going to take for our country to realize that what the founding fathers meant by "Pursuit of Happiness" and our interpretation of this pursuit today are vastly different beasts.

I am so very grateful to work with many people who do not pursue their own happiness. If you are a leader of others (and quite frankly that is everyone), and you pursue your own happiness to the point where it is more important than pursuing goodness or, say faithfulness, then you may find yourself very alone one day.

I am pleased to inform you that there is a counter-movement to our own constitution and you can easily become a part of it. We must stop pursuing our own happiness and realize that a truer and purer form of happiness exists when we pursue the well-being of others.

This altruistic look at life seems almost archaic to a modern world that insists we deserve something more. It is quite refreshing to work with people who have come to realize that they don't deserve anything, but rather see their lives as blessings and turn their attention towards helping others.

For those of you who have found this brand of happiness, keep giving it away. Do not hoard it. If you are still in pursuit of happiness in your job, in your family, with your friends or in any other walk of your life, I recommend you get off that road and get on the one that pursues authentic care for others.

We must not be conformed to this pattern the world has sold us. A different train is leaving the station — all aboard!

From Fear to Care

When I take the time to consider just how rapidly the world is changing, sometimes I can get flat out scared. Fear is a funny thing, and the way that it manifests itself in people is amazingly diverse. I am convinced that if you live and breathe, you have some fear. Perhaps you don't have a full blown phobia, but there is bound to be something that makes you uneasy or even keeps you up at night.

One good thing to do if you catch yourself living with fear is to name the fear — that is, identify it clearly. Sometimes I fear the changing world because I think that if I don't understand all of the changes, the world will somehow leave me behind and I will be as irrelevant and obsolete as a vinyl record player. By understanding and "naming" the nature of this fear, I allow myself to step aside and take a more objective look at what is really happening. This identification and objective assessment rarely fails me in quelling my fear. When I get to this point, to keep from slipping back into that fear, I often ask myself if there is something bigger than my fear that I can focus on, something that will not become obsolete. What I keep coming back to is the one surefire thing that will never be outdated and will always be something the world needs more of: authentic care for others. No technological breakthroughs, deteriorating economy or global political issue will ever overshadow the need for you to authentically and selflessly care for other people. Once I get back to this REALITY, and begin to act upon it, I have effectively beaten back the fear. Try it — the world will be a better place when you do.

Give and Take

Every year around the holidays, my family and I have a discussion about not making the presents our focus. And yet every year, we still kind of do. I once heard a speaker who kept referring to us (the general public) as "consumers." The more he said it, the more I got offended. I understand that economically that is what we are. But I kept getting put off by the idea that he was saying it as if it was our identity. We are consumers. How offensive.

I couldn't shake the idea that a consumer was one who just took and took and took and gave nothing back. Frankly, I just don't want to be that guy. We are more than consumers. Or should I say, we have the capacity to be more than consumers.

Every time you buy something, a good question to ask is "What am I giving back?" You could be at the grocery store and all you have to give back is a smile or a kind word. What an amazing world we all create if every time we thought about "consuming" we would also think about giving.

Generosity and thoughtful actions are the antidote to being just consumers. The world in which we live needs way more givers than consumers. Give with your resources, give with your time, or give with your words — but give something.

Our culture doesn't esteem giving so much anymore — which is primarily why we are now just "consumers." I understand that to keep our economy going in the right direction we need to consume, but I can't understand why we couldn't adopt enough awareness to give of ourselves with equal fervor.

A Numbers Game

How many times have you heard that sales is a "numbers game?" It's funny how some things can become so cliché that we don't take the time to stop and consider the truth or untruth behind the euphemism. So what do you think? Is it a numbers game or isn't it?

From my chair, I would say that this quip is absolutely true — but needs a brief addition or we simply go astray. I suggest 'effective selling is about diligence to the numbers coupled with authentically caring about people.' There are some strategies that would absolutely ignore the last piece about caring for others and just teach the numbers piece — make enough calls, write enough notes, meet enough people, and you win. And, I must admit that I have actually seen this work.

What I want to propose, however, is that if you couple the humanity part with the numbers game, you will be amongst the elite in sales. Ironically, many people have a difficult time playing just the "numbers." There is something at a soul level that knows it should be more than just mindlessly encountering as many people as possible.

If you have recently considered how you may increase your sales, go back to the basics of playing the numbers game. Add into your mix the human trait of authentic care and you will find success.

Can I Trust You?

Trust is everything. Without it, your business will flounder, your relationships will go nowhere and almost every area of your life will be impacted.

This idea is not new, but in today's topsy-turvy world it is increasingly evident. Many of my clients are doing very well in their businesses. For some, their success has seemed almost inexplicable. Calls are coming in from every direction. How do we explain why certain individuals thrive and others don't?

The common denominator I am seeing in those who have an abundance of business right now is that they have spent their careers building systems and teams designed to authentically help people. As a result, people trust them. Regardless of what industry you are in, I beg you not to underestimate this trait. Building trust with people could be the most critical aspect of your business and life success.

It's a little problematic, however, because trust cannot be built or earned overnight. Rather, it is a position of your heart that is acted out every day.

Trust is not something you can fake — well, maybe you can fake it for a while, but you will see that it won't get you very far. Care enough about people to speak the truth. Increase your knowledge about what is going on so that you can use your knowledge to help others make wise decisions. Care more about others than you do about making a sale. These are actions which build trust over time.

It is my prediction that as the world gets increasingly unpredictable, trust will become all the more critical. Go care!

Practicing Fakeness

Somewhere on our long and winding roads we have encountered a critic — perhaps more than one. A critic who felt bad enough about themselves to cast judgment on us, and who left us writhing in self-doubt and shame. The result was that we are now often stymied by a strange sense of perfectionism — a perfectionism that can cause us to avoid the type of interaction that is necessary for our jobs.

We battle the need to be perfect because we fear the same sense of impending judgment that has riddled our souls for years. I coach many people who continue to suffer from this form of perfectionism, which is extremely unhealthy and unproductive. Some have even come to believe that they do not have anything of real substance to offer the world. In their own minds, if they are going to have to create relationships, or go out and "sell", then they simply must "fake it till they make it." Sometimes the fear and anxiety of getting out and creating relationships is so real that the only strategy some people can think to deploy is faking it. I have seen and heard some amazing fakers — but I have a better way.

Start with forgiving all of the people who ever criticized you in a way that diminished your true talent. Then take a moment and realize that you will never be perfect, but that you do have something great to bring to the world. The greatest sales call you may ever make is the one where you practice authentic, careful listening. Do not try and feign authenticity — either you care or you don't.

We live in a world that desperately needs your authentic heart. If you do authentically care, then go out with abandon. Take your imperfections and all — and go. What most people need is someone who takes an earnest interest in them and sees them for the beauty and creativity that they bring to the world.

Marianne Williamson noted that "As we are liberated from our own fears, our presence automatically liberates others." Be caged no more — make today great!

Touchy-Feely Malarkey

Business is about making money. All of this talk about having a deep purpose and creating authentic relationships is a bunch of hooey. I do what I do because I need to make cash. I have bills to pay.

I have heard this kind of talk for years: the idea that focusing on anything but money in business is nothing but fluff. Interestingly, the people from the "in it for the money" camp are not entirely wrong. This is what makes this argument so tricky. Some people espouse the 'money' theory, but in a very roundabout fashion. They may not admit it, but it is at the heart of everything they do. All attempts to claim anything different are but shadow truths. If pressed, they will usually admit that business is primarily about making money.

There is a mountain of science to prove that money itself is not an effective motivator. But those whose hearts are already calibrated in that direction may not listen anyway.

Recently a friend sent me the hierarchy of needs by Abraham Maslow. In 1943, Dr. Maslow created a simple pyramid-style diagram to illustrate how human needs are met. The higher you go on the needs list, the more you evolve as a human.

Money and material needs made the list, but they are low on the proverbial totem pole. If we are to evolve into a better version of who we are designed to be, we must break out of the thought that money is all we need. You wouldn't tell your clients that money is your number one need. If you did, why would they want to do business with you?

When many around us feel the pangs of a broken economy, they may fall down in the hierarchy of needs. Money is important, but if you want to have more, put your focus on something other than just acquiring it. Simply making lots of money won't inspire anyone. We all need to wake up and realize that inspiring others is a higher priority than making money. Let us do our best to search for our authentic heart and its true motivation.

Reverse Learning

Customer service has long been the subject of study and focus for almost every company I can think of. No other business topic is so overanalyzed, to the point that if we hear one more lesson about "service," we cynically turn away. And yet, with all of that, service is something that is still so amazingly void in real life.

Have you been on an airplane lately? Have you run through the gauntlet of uncaring, uninspired, unenthusiastic people that are part of anything that has to do with air travel? I was recently sitting on a plane, marveling at the lack of anything that remotely resembled "customer service," while I listened to the pre-recorded announcement of the CEO of that airline. He was telling us that service was one of their top priorities! For a moment I thought I was in a *Twilight Zone* episode. But then I thought to myself, 'What can I observe and learn from their behavior?'

Sad as it may seem, I started to realize that you could observe most of the people from the front counter, through TSA, and on to the actual plane, and simply practice the opposite behaviors to create a wonderful platform for bringing service to your organization. I know it seems disparaging, but the lessons I learned about how NOT to do something were actually quite revealing! It was a great help to my attitude as well which, if I'm being honest, is in the toilet most of the time when I'm traveling.

So I have made it a point to "reverse learn." The lessons are incredible.

One thing I have found is that there are always diamonds in the rough. There is, on occasion, an individual who helps and cares, simply because that's the kind of person they wish to be. We should recognize those people for their efforts in such a dismal world. In fact, I would call us to BE those people. Authentically caring — irrespective of what anyone tells you "customer service" should be — is the backbone of it all. Do that and the rest will fall into place.

Catch and Release

I love fishing. Some people enjoy being in the mountains, on a beach, or in the desert, but for me there's something about being near a stream that brings peace. The type of fishing I love the most is fly-fishing for trout. Since I don't particularly like the taste of trout, I use the method called "catch and release." (Even if you have never fished before, I'm sure this method requires no further explanation.)

It struck me that "catch and release" is also what we need to do with our possessions. It is when we catch and hold that we get into trouble. I know that I hold on too tightly to the things I have. My home, my cars, and my money all have too much importance and command too much of my time and attention.

Today, I want to offer a suggestion that could be a huge blessing for you: make this season the most generous and giving of your life. Find a charity, a friend, a church, or a stranger, and help them. Let go of something you cherish and give it to someone less fortunate.

Then, don't make a big deal out of it. Simply do it from your heart. Wherever you are, there is a food bank, homeless shelter, or soup kitchen that is working hard to help others. Now, it is quite likely you have caught some incredible fish in your life. Even if you feel that you are struggling right now, if you are reading this, I tell you that you are blessed — and that you can bless others by what you have caught.

This is a rough season for many people. By using the "catch and release" method in life, you will paradoxically receive even more.

You will not find the power of this lesson in any economics class. But I promise you that when you loosen your grip and release some of what you have, you will be amazed at what comes back to you. Wouldn't it be great to be a master "catch and releaser?"

We Will Never Do Great Things

Mother Teresa of Calcutta was an Albanian-born Catholic nun whose life was so revered that today she has become a euphemism in our country for perfection. Hence, when we fall short, we say "Well, I'm no Mother Teresa." I came across a quote by an incredible woman who apparently didn't think she was a "Mother Teresa" either. She said, "None of us, including me, ever do great things. But we can all do small things, with great love, and together we can do something wonderful."

I have coached many people who certainly don't feel like Mother Teresa. But this woman only accomplished amazing things by doing the small actions over and over again. We all overcomplicate our lives and our businesses. While I do believe that there is a time for ambitious plans and amazingly creative visions, sometimes what we really need is to do some small things consistently.

Oh, and let's not forget the "with great love" part. If that sounds too squishy for you, get over it. If our lives and our businesses were a sum total of consistent small actions done out of love, it is likely we would have all the success we could handle.

I thought about ending by stating that you don't actually have to be Mother Teresa, but then I realized that she herself called every one of us to do just that. These were her words which I quoted above. She is the very woman who urges us to take small actions.

So, actually, you do possess the power to be exactly like Mother Teresa. Your calling may not involve saving thousands of starving, homeless children on the streets of Calcutta. But whatever you are doing, your small acts of love will elevate you in profound ways. Try it. If I'm wrong, then what harm done? I doubt I'll get any angry e-mails about anyone having done too many little things with too much love.

IMPROVE YOUR HEALTH

Let us all stop buying the lie that we simply don't have time to stay healthy.

Take Back Your Health

I was sick recently with a pretty significant sinus infection. As a lifelong learner, I try to draw lessons from all situations in life, and that includes illness. If there is one lesson I took away from this infectious bout, it is this: don't get sick. Of course I am being partly facetious. But the truth is that I often take my health for granted. I feel blessed that, for the most part, I am a healthy person.

Are you? Do you take your health for granted?

Being proactive with your physical health could be one of the single greatest contributions to your own success, and it's one that you have control over. But, alas, so many people get so busy that staying healthy just doesn't fit into their calendar. The sad irony is that, when we are not intentional about our health, we often lose it. Then we grit our teeth at the fact that we can't do much to serve the world while we're nursing ourselves on a couch. Of course, staying healthy by working out, eating clean, and getting enough rest is not some guaranteed way to never get hurt or sick, but it sure helps.

There is a vicious cycle that goes like this: We go through a season where we don't make health a priority, and then we get sick or hurt. While we are sick or hurt we are rendered less effective, which leads to anxiety and stress. Anxiety and stress lead to a whole host of other issues, not the least of which are poor sleep and work habits. This leads us right back to not having enough time to work out and stay healthy.

How about that merry-go-round? Put an end to the cycle by doing what you can to stay physically healthy. Put health as a priority in your calendar.

So many positive things happen when we feel good and our bodies are well rested. We must stop buying the lie that we don't have time.

Stressful Rest

There has been a common theme in my coaching lately: stress and a lack of rest. I have had too many clients express a frustration with a lack of sleep, and an increase of stress during their day. The funny thing is that stress itself can create a hindrance to sleep. Then, when we are sleep deprived, we have a propensity to get more stressed during the day. Where does that vicious cycle end?

To be honest, it ends with illness. Often this combination of little rest and high stress crushes our immune system until we get a cold or the flu or something worse. Stress is attributed to many serious diseases, but since it is so difficult to correlate the two, folks often just go on living their stress-filled lives until some sort of sickness forces them to shut down.

The real issue for me is that there is no plan of tangible action to stop being stressed. Can you imagine that? Coach: "Hey stop being stressed by this Friday." Client: "Sounds good, thanks, Coach. By the way, got any ideas about how I can do that?"

I do have some ideas about how to reduce stress in one's life. But for the moment, I simply wanted to throw this irony out there to see if it could get our minds to embrace the Catch 22. I am always intrigued by events in life that pose a conundrum.

I have many clients and friends who are just not getting proper rest and are leading lives that are horribly stressed, day in and day out. I could point out that exercise and meditation or prayer are good antidotes to this, but frankly most people don't have the time for either of these. They're too "busy" doing all of the things that cause the stress and lack of sleep.

I sometimes have daydreams that this idea might start a revolution. Imagine a group of people all geared up to fight for the cause of good rest and a stress-reduced lifestyle. If it does indeed start a movement, I hope someone else is the leader. I am too busy, and that would stress me out!

Choose Health

"If we do not make time for health today, we will be forced to take the time for illness later."

The best coaching I can give someone who is sick is to "get better." That may sound obvious, but you might be surprised how often we just don't heed that advice. We keep plugging ahead, and it only compounds the issue. If you are feeling well today and want to keep it that way, I have just two recommendations.

1. Be very attentive to your level of stress.

A stress-filled life is an immune system killer. No, I am not a doctor. But when I am coaching someone who is highly stressed, they seem to be always teetering on the edge of a bad cold or flu. Stress has a much greater impact on us than we realize. This is especially true for those of us who think that we are better than the average person at handling it — and let's face it, that includes most of us. There are hundreds of techniques to deal with stress. But the awareness alone may help you lower its effects.

2. Exercise.

A healthy body makes for a healthy immune system. Ironically, the number one reason many people don't exercise is time. When we don't exercise, we are forced to a screeching halt by illness. Then we get behind — which means no time for exercise — and we plug ahead madly until another illness takes us out.

You can stop this vicious cycle. Recommit yourself to a plan today, even if it means beginning with a few small steps.

You don't have time to be sick. Instead, choose to invest your time in pursuing health. You'll feel better every day, and you'll get a lot more enjoyment out of your free time.

4 Ways to Mitigate Stress

Stress, like pain, is completely subjective. I have always found it fascinating when a doctor asks me to rate my pain on a scale of 1-10.

How would he know if my 8 isn't someone else's 3? Or vice versa? Similarly, stress impacts us all so variedly. Some people do a good job of managing it, so that you may not see all of its ugly by-products (yet). Those who don't manage it well may reveal all of its nasty manifestations on a daily basis. But in the long run, stress is bad for you, whether you manage it well or not.

Here are four tips for limiting stress. It is my hope that at least one of them will be of help to you:

Exercise regularly. If you are already doing this, you may want to consider increasing the time or intensity or simply changing your routine. For example, I love to run, but my wife and I took a Yoga class. It was painful and challenging, but a fantastic change to the routine.

Pay attention to the amount and quality of sleep you get. This can be tough, because it may be stress that is causing a lack of sleep. Even so, it is important to make sleep a priority. Burning the candles at both ends is destructive. Sleep is a great builder of your immune system.

Pray and meditate. So many of us know the power of prayer and meditation, but strangely we put it in the backseat when we are busy.

Take daily vacations. Practice the art of being done when you are done. When you go home in the evening, BE home.

If you implement these four tips, you will find that each one feeds the others. Exercise helps to refresh your mind so that you can be more present. Prayer and meditation can help ease the way to more restful sleep. When you are more rested, you'll find that sticking to an exercise routine is easier. And so on… Let us end the madness of incessant stress. The longevity and quality of your life may hang in the balance.

Breaking Through

If I were asked to identify the single greatest problem that most people in our culture face today, both at work and at home, I would say that it is busyness. Our lives seem to be a collection of decisions: Should I do this or that? Go here or there? Make this call or that one? Should I join this group or that one? Should my kid play this sport or that? In the end, often the answer that we think will save us is to say "yes" to all of it! And as we attempt to do it all, we lament our unending busyness.

Most people are so exhausted that they can't even bring themselves to seek out a possible solution. If that is you, I'm so sorry. I am diving into the deep end. Consider the possibility that the real issue is something beyond busyness. Perhaps the issue is that we fear losing something.

We fear losing a relationship, a business deal, a phone call, and certainly we fear losing money. We fear that we will be missing out on something great if we say "no" to anything. So, we say "yes" to everything. We take on a spirit of incessant busyness. This leads to stress and anxiety, which in turn leads to things like lack of sleep, illness, irritability, and a host of other problems.

If this is even close to defining your reality, I want you to know there is hope. But the hope begins with your choices. I believe we must be willing to let go of the fear of loss. We must confront the fact that not doing every possible activity will NOT lead to our destruction. It really is ok to say "no" to some things. In fact, your peace and prosperity may depend on it.

The ultimate answer is certainly not to say "no" to everything — that would be an over-correction. It may be as simple as realizing that bad things won't happen if you don't take on everything right now. Let us all be discerning about the root cause of the busyness. Major life breakthroughs will happen as a result.

Practice Peace

Do what you can, with what you have, for whom you can, in the time that you allot... and then practice peace. I have many clients right now who, in the spirit of seizing the day and working hard, are simply going overboard with how much they are trying to accomplish. It isn't that I haven't seen amazing abilities to execute many things, but when we attempt to do more than we should, for the people we shouldn't, we experience burnout. I am all about the soft-skill of work ethic; truthfully some of us need to develop more of it. But today, stress is at an all-time high.

I simply don't have the ability to list out all the detriments of stress, so here's a simple reminder: a stress-filled life will harm you.

The antidote comes back to saying "yes" when we can and "no" when we should. In increasingly difficult times we believe that we should say yes to almost everything, thinking that yes means more sales, more relationships, and more production. In almost every case saying "yes" to the wrong people in the wrong circumstances means not meeting expectations, frustration and stress. The act of abundance today is being more and more clear about who, when, and where you can help. After that, step back and know that you have done all that you should have. Practice the art of peace.

Simplificity

When someone says to me, "Don't worry," I think to myself, "How can I not worry when worrying comes as naturally to me as breathing?" I can appreciate the concept of "don't worry," and I do understand the benefits. I just wish that advice came with instructions.

I've noticed a similar idea hitting the radar in coaching, and so I carefully thought over how to write about it. The advice goes something like this: "You must simplify your life." Now, that may seem like sage advice. It may sound very appealing, refreshing even… but how do you do it? How can you just simplify?

Like so many other topics, the answer to that may require deeper thought. The answer — if it is even a question for you — may require some meditation, some questioning, and a willingness to be still enough to hear the answers.

I don't know too many people that couldn't benefit from some form of simplification. I've seen a growing number of clients begin to experience the awful byproducts of complicated living. So many of us have a tendency to pile more and more stuff into our lives, and we need to learn our limits and say no to a few things.

Yes, contrary to popular motivational mumbo jumbo, we do have limits. By actually limiting the activities in our lives, we give ourselves a better chance at being great by mastering the few things we should be doing.

This takes both courage and discernment — the courage to say no to some things and yes to others, and the discernment to know which is which.

Engaging in the right amount of activity will help us in our quest for simplification, and it can go a great way toward reducing stress. Reducing stress can go a long way toward bringing peace and health. Ah… more Hope for our inevitable Reality!

Consider this quote by German artist Hans Hofmann: "The ability to simplify means to eliminate the unnecessary so that the necessary may speak."

Justifiable

Who you are and what you do when no one is watching makes a difference. Stop for a moment and consider your own character. There are countless components, and some are probably very positive. You may be a kind and generous person. You may be thoughtful and intelligent. It is worth reflecting on the good characteristics that help make up the complex individuals that we are. The most successful people, however, are always digging for those areas that they need to improve. Too many people look in the mirror and justify themselves exactly as they are. They essentially throw up their hands and accept themselves, flaws and all. This is one of many ways we evade the tough discipline of taking a good honest look at who we really are, what we are doing with our time, and what needs to change.

It is gut-wrenching to really examine our own actions and motives. It is tough to admit that we are not where and who we want to be. It is even more painful to stop justifying our actions or blaming our circumstances, and admit that we hold within us the power to change.

What is it that needs to change in your life? Do you need to change an eating pattern? Do you need to change what you look at on the internet? Do you need to change your attitude toward someone in your life? Do you need to change how you view your job? Large or small, we all have things that we need to improve if we are going to live the life we desire. Let us stop justifying bad behavior. Instead, let's seek the courage to change.

The best don't ever stop asking what they can do to improve who they are.

Walls

When you think of a wall, what is the first thing that comes to your mind? Do you think of a barrier? A dividing line? Protection? Boundaries? If you build a wall around you for self-protection, it can also be a barrier that stops people from helping and guiding you. In this case, walls are not good.

The Great Wall of China — though monumental and beautiful now — once represented a great rift between tribes and dynasties. Ronald Reagan implored Mikhail Gorbachev to "tear down" the Berlin wall, which represented hate and conflict between two worlds.

But there are some walls that need construction or renovation.

The wall that represents boundaries around your disciplines needs to be fortified over and over again. The wall that protects our hearts from the inevitable evil in the world must be strong. The wall that guards the commitments that we make in our lives must be powerful and able to withstand many hits.

Our lives have many metaphors, and walls can represent something reprehensible or something necessary and good. Let us tear down the walls that divide us and keep us apart — but at the same time, let us construct and fortify the ones that guard our hearts and keep us within healthy boundaries.

If you think of your life and business commitments as a wall that cannot be torn down, you will do well. If you think you can be free by removing all boundaries, you may find yourself in a prison of your own making. Live in the true freedom that springs from the commitments and boundaries around us.

CHALLENGES COME

Resilience may be one of the most relevant characteristics a person needs in order to navigate through the rapidly-changing waters of business and life.

From Darkness Comes…

I believe one of the great travesties of our society is our unwillingness to look into our own story and claim that the darker parts of our lives are integral to the overall pilgrimage to who we really are.

It seems that our country refuses to allow that there are true hardships in our lives and that those hardships are actually a major part of what shapes us into whole beings. We live in a world that simply does not accept suffering as part of the journey.

Has it ever occurred to us that this country may actually have to go through pain before it can experience the freedom upon which it was founded? Our pain avoidance and bailout mindset is doing little more than ushering in a longer, deeper pain than we need.

It's not that I can't appreciate the soul's desire to not be in travail. It's rather that we may be going too far in avoidance of pain to remember that most true joy, success, peace and authentic love come only after one owns the idea that life is ripe with both good and bad, light and darkness. To pretend and pose as if our stories didn't have a painful part of the journey is to live only half a life.

I believe we can serve the world better by being transparent about this. I do not believe we need to linger in the dark parts of our lives, but we all have to journey through them in order to be complete.

The Twin Thieves

"Know thy enemy." Sometime around 500 BC, the legendary Chinese military commander Sun Tzu penned this well-known quote in his work The Art of War. He goes on to explain further that, if you don't know who or what your enemy is, you could get taken out by something you didn't even know existed. There are many enemies today. Some are more tangible than others. Regardless of whether you see the "enemy" like I do, I believe we would be foolish to not consider the enemy's ways.

For the sake of being succinct, I will borrow words from Robert Hastings' poem "The Station" when he said that "regret and fear are twin thieves who would rob us of today." I believe this effectively sums up two key methods the enemy uses against us. The first "thief" is fear. The degree to which we live in fear determines so much about how we walk through this life. We all have fears (snakes, heights, fear of loss) and some are more reasonable than others.

Fear runs rampant today in our culture and is wreaking havoc on the best of people. Recognizing fear as the enemy and battling fear with hope and awareness can be a game-changer for you.

The other "thief" is the twin sibling of fear: regret. When we spend time pondering the many things we could have and should have done, we are robbing ourselves of doing the things we can do today. Regret is conquered by action. We must know these enemies or, like Sun Tzu says, we will "succumb in every battle." Be in the present today, and serve as many as you can with your work and your life. Do this and you will have successfully fought back against the twin thieves. No Fear. No Regret.

Make a Wish

The great Jim Rohn said many wonderful things. He was a walking, talking source of wisdom in simple snippets. Jim's book *Leading an Inspired Life* is one of my all-time favorites. The quote that I hope we can all grasp is as follows: "Don't wish that things were easier, wish instead that you were better."

It is so very common to wish that things were easier. Your life, your work, your relationships... difficult situations are all around us.

But there is a trap we can fall into when we simply wish that our circumstances were different. It is very possible that things will not get any easier any time soon. Working on our hearts and making personal improvements may be the only viable option.

What has caused you frustration recently, and left you wishing it was different? Are you frustrated by the economy? Frustrated by the government? Have changes to your job caused you to become bitter? For too many people the answer has been a resounding YES!

You may be right as rain about some of the difficulties, but in the midst of arduous times you can make a personal choice to curtail the lamenting and simply get on with making a choice to be better within your circumstances. It is one of the great acts of personal responsibility to face the wind and take action. It will be difficult, but if you look around, you will find others who are doing it.

Let us join them and stay on the quest of betterment as we navigate volatile times.

Changes

A client once commented to me that she felt like she was sitting in the front row of human history, watching the world change in unbelievable ways. Of course, it's nearly impossible to encounter change purely as a spectator. Change does funny things to people. Some welcome it with open arms, while others fight it, kicking and biting the whole way.

Regardless of how you handle change, I recommend that you first embrace the fact that you must go through it. I have observed that some people are resisting change altogether, and their resistance can be fatal. So here's a thought: just because you have a strategy, technique, or tactic that worked for you in the past, there is no guarantee that it will work for you today.

Certainly there are times to use discernment and stay on a certain course. However, when your environment changes, you must often advance in a different direction. For example, what you say when you speak to your clients in a time of crisis verses what you said to them in a more stable environment may be entirely different. I am coaching virtually every one of my clients to embrace the change around them, and then to help the people in their lives to do the same.

The "courage to change the things you can" part of the Serenity Prayer refers directly to your willingness to change yourself in any given circumstance.

Let's all get on board!

Resilience

Resilience is a developable quality. It may be one of the most important and relevant characteristics a person needs today in order to navigate through the rapidly-changing waters of business and life. I used to believe that only a certain behavioral pattern resisted change. But I am finding that just about every single person I know resists changing. And when certain changes are forced upon us, we can become bitter, hardened and stubborn.

Being resilient means that you find a way to step up every day and keep going even in the face of circumstances that make you change your ways.

To be sure, there are times in which you must discern what you will fight for and what you will accept. Lately, I am finding many clients dig their heels in, simply because they would rather fight the tide than make a change. A change to their thinking or a change to the way they conduct themselves day to day. This is particularly hard when you have convinced yourself that the way you have always done things is the 'right way' or the only way that works.

The fear we all have in accepting the fact that we actually can go down another path is staggering. I am not insinuating that some things don't need to be fought for — they do. I'm simply saying that I have seen progress made when we face that fear and go in another direction.

So what do you need to accept today? What has changed in your world at work or home that is calling you to change with it? Where do you find yourself defending your way, your style and your program? In this ever-changing environment, it would be virtually impossible to think you don't need to accept some level of change. It could be that one little thing you do, the one call you make or simply accepting the fact that you can make a change.

You are much more resilient than you may know. The small changes you have to make will do you good.

Mountains and Molehills

I am a student of human interactivity. As a coach, I have the privilege of being able to partake in countless human interactions, responses, and activities every day. I used to think quite arrogantly that one day I would understand it all. Now I know I never will. There are simply too many variables in life to ever really "figure it out."

One such variable is change itself. Observing how people (myself included) deal with change has been fascinating. Some deal quite well, while others really struggle. In today's world, change is happening at breakneck speed and its impact is far-reaching. This ever-changing environment can cause us to make small challenges bigger than they should be. I see this trap repeated over and over again.

If you find yourself fixating on a problem, notice how much time you spend thinking about it and trying to solve it. When you are in that mode, remember that there are much bigger more important aspects of your life that are being ignored.

I am not implying that these small issues are unimportant. But I have noticed that we often give them too much attention. When so much time and effort is spent, the problem only magnifies itself.

The love of your family and friends, your vocation, your health — these things need your attention too. Let's not allow some of the molehills in life to derail us from our purpose!

Veer Right

Change is in the air. For some this is welcome, but for others change represents an uncertain and frightening new place. If you are in a season that requires change for your own benefit, I want to encourage you to lean in and make the decision to go down that road... before you are dragged there by force.

A fork in the road is the perfect metaphor for the decisions we must face so frequently in our lives. And yet many of the forks aren't 90 degree turns, but rather gentle bends that carry us in a different direction. Yes, the new direction may be unknown to you, but it is possible that staying on the path you are comfortable with could gradually lead to disaster.

It is my hope that you are thinking of a specific situation and a specific change you should make right now. When you come to that fork, it is always good to stop and consider, meditate or pray about the new road. Certainly you should weigh your options and get council from a trusted advisor. But should you decide to take the road less travelled, remember that your actions don't always have to be a U-turn or a monumental shift. You may just need to veer to the right with some intentionality. Some of life's greatest blessings and successes have come from small, gradual shifts.

Unearthing Opportunities

Anytime you feel a large group of people (perhaps even a whole nation) complaining or otherwise lamenting a common topic, never forget that there is almost always an opportunity planted along side. If, for example, there are some regulatory changes that have an entire industry on edge, don't forget that there is usually a huge opportunity to educate while others bellyache.

We don't always have to agree with changes to be able to turn them into positives for our businesses and our lives. There are a tremendous amount of laws and statutes being developed as a result of the economy — many seem to lack any common sense at all. Still, understanding these changes, and helping those who don't, can give you a leg up. Educating others for their benefit will do nothing but help you establish greater trust with your clients. Trust is everything in business and it is the foundation to all relationship selling.

There is a time to take a stand and fight for honesty and fairness in our laws; there is also a time to know what the changes are and how they impact you (and others) so that you can help your clients navigate through difficult times.

If you find yourself on the complaining side of things, please remember that an opportunity usually sits nearby.

Don't Fester

Life is a series of moments. Many of them are filled with joy, beauty, and contentment. But some of our moments are wrought with frustration, resentment and anger. Going through these moments is all too human. I have yet to meet someone who doesn't experience these things. Unfortunately, when some of us get to that point, we stay there. We fester.

I intentionally chose the word "fester" because it evokes imagery that is grotesque. We get stuck in that ugly moment. There is a way out, even when you feel like there isn't. There is a way to stop the festering and get the train back on the tracks. It does require a bit of self-awareness, but here's the trick: when you are gripped by the anxieties of life, don't ask "What can I do?" but rather "Who can I call or visit right now?"

Irrespective of your circumstances, there are people around you who absolutely need you right now. A simple call, a quick visit — turning your focus to someone else — could be just the thing to dislodge you from your self-made prison. I often remind my clients that a key role in their job description is "Inspirer of Others." You don't have to be John Maxwell or Zig Ziglar to carry the title of Inspirer. You may need to remember, however, that festering too long in negative circumstances makes it virtually impossible to inspire others.

Finding yourself in that "festering moment" is human. Getting out of it is a choice. You have an amazing capacity to end your own festering. Go make that call.

Beating a Spirit

"I am so busy!" This utterance is so commonplace that it has become the cry of the 21st century. Most people I know are so busy that they are missing out on aspects of their lives that they would ordinary deem too important to neglect. I do realize that some of the busyness is positive and productive. I would never coach someone to simply drop everything and go live in a cave. However, I think it is entirely reasonable to suggest that we all take time to stop and evaluate our busyness.

The evaluation itself is quite simple. Ask yourself: is my day-to-day so jammed with urgent activity that I am simply not doing some activities that are important?

Urgent vs. important — this is so crucial. If we don't start looking at what is important to us, it is quite possible that there will be an end result that we simply didn't imagine.

I detest writing things that sound like a threat. However, in my estimation, this spirit of busyness is going to hurt many people. Key relationships and our own physical and mental health are being put aside so that we can pile on more and more urgency. All this urgency eventually leads us to a reactive existence. It's life-sucking when gone unchecked.

I say, take a break and evaluate. Be honest with yourself. Be willing to look at the choices you are making, and if indeed you see that you are missing the important accounts in your life, be willing to make new choices. There is a wonderful and challenging Proverb that says this: "All a man's ways seem right to him..." (Proverbs 21:2) This is the danger. Nobody thinks that their choices are wrong — at least, not in that moment. Only through transparent evaluation could we actually see that some of this busyness is a lethal blind spot.

I implore you to reflect and have the courage to make a different choice if you need to. Let's get back on track with what is truly important, and not get sucked into the vortex of busyness. There is a better way...

Planned Obstacles

We all have seasons when things are operating well, systems are playing out smoothly, and all seems right with the world. In these times, we are like a runner who is peacefully jogging around a smooth track with no obstacles in our way. If you're not in that place today, odds are you are trying to get there. But even when you arrive in that zone, there are inevitable barriers not far off. I say this not to be pessimistic, but rather to offer some hope to those of us who seem to be running a steeplechase rather than a smooth track.

In athletics, the steeplechase is a fascinating race because it purposefully makes the runners leap over barriers, sometimes landing in a puddle of water. Many of my clients are running the steeplechase in business and in life. Some of them choose to accept and even expect the barriers, while others can't seem to understand why they are there or what they're supposed to do.

Your life and your business will have obstacles — that should not come as a surprise. What amazes me is that, when turns, leaps, and landings come, some of us embrace them while others refuse to engage. It got me thinking about the athletes that train for this type of race. When they are on the course, the barriers and pits are part of the circuit. Because there is no way to remove the obstacles, they work very hard at being able to effectively and quickly surmount them.

Some of us are still fighting the fact that we are not running on flat ground. This fight can create even more stress than the obstacles themselves. If you are in a season in your business or your life where there are traps, difficulties and snags… embrace them, expect them, and train as if they are just around the corner.

Don't forget that you possess an uncanny ability to work through these changes and hardships. One of the best ways to conquer them is to recognize that most of life isn't smooth sailing, and expect more challenges ahead.

Train for them, and you will see that there are no hurdles you can't get over.

Neither Wind, Nor Rain, Nor Snow...

Four times each year, I traveled to the quarterly meeting of The Masters' Coach, a Building Champions group that I had been involved with for many years. It was exciting each time I got to be with this posse! Unfortunately, there always seemed to be a few who couldn't join us because of the challenges life threw their way.

It meant so much to me to be a part of a group of people who came together for the common purpose of sharing and learning from each other. When you engage with others, you feel more fully alive. You are more connected, and your actions take on greater meaning.

But there is always resistance.

At times, there may have been literal storms hammering our country that cancelled flights and kept some from attending. People in the group had also been taken out by things like injury, illness, and personal loss.

Storms of all kinds can hit our lives and cause us to stay grounded. If you want to ensure that you are maximizing your life, then you cannot let these forces pull you too far off course or too far away from the very people that can help you.

When the challenges are the greatest, and when you feel the most like pulling away from the world, that is the very time when you must engage with the greatest intention. Sure, there are risks, but the returns so far outweigh the risks that it would be crazy to remain disengaged.

Over the years, some members of The Masters' Coach had faced difficult and even tragic circumstances. And every time they engaged amid those challenges, I witnessed others in the group surrounding them with support and comfort.

Don't let the storms of life hold you back.

Keep engaging!

Fortitude

One definition of the word fortitude is "strength of mind that allows one to endure pain or adversity with courage." I am encountering more and more situations that call for greater levels of fortitude. Now I realize that you may be in a really good spot. If this defines you today, then by all means keep going — do not stop or allow complacency to creep in and block your forward progress. Your action plan is to ride the wave of momentum that you have created.

If, however, your current season of life is defined more by challenges, roadblocks and difficulties, then perhaps what you need is nothing shy of a dose of fortitude.

Let us never forget that some of the greatest thinkers and spiritual giants that ever walked the earth spoke about the necessity of challenging times. One of life's greatest ironies is that we try so fervently to avoid the challenges and pitfalls, only to realize these are the very things which forge our character.

As I gaze around today, I see many colleagues, clients and friends whose current journey is marked more by obstacles than anything else. The track they are on looks more like a steeplechase than a flat, smooth surface. While I wouldn't wish these challenges upon anyone, I can tell you that this course is creating in many of these people a stronger spirit and an unmistakable quality that will serve them for the remainder of their lives.

Every one of us has been given a greater dose of strength to carry on than we often realize. Embedded in the fabric of your being is the power to do amazing things, even in the midst of what appears like an endless storm. Nobel Prize-winning author William Faulkner said, "People need trouble — a little frustration to sharpen the spirit on, toughen it. Artists do; I don't mean you need to live in a rat hole or gutter, but you have to learn fortitude, endurance. Only vegetables are happy."

Go be great, irrespective of your circumstances.

One Eye Up

It is challenging to think you can write anything that is going to reach the masses. Our lives have become increasingly complex, and it isn't as if we all move at the same speed. Some of my clients right now are doing very well, and others are in the struggle of their life. Perhaps this is the way it has always been.

If you feel like you are in the midst of a difficult battle, I want to offer a bit of coaching to you. When times get rough, a very natural, very human thing to do is to put your head down and just try and get through the day.

Now, sometimes keeping your head down and working at the task at hand is a good thing. But if you keep your head down too long, you'll forget where you were headed. As challenging as it may seem to you today, you need to look up and take note of where you are going. I am speaking about reviewing, revising, rejuvenating, or even creating your Vision.

"Where there is no vision, the people perish," claims the good King Solomon. (Proverbs 29:18) The number one issue with creating or updating a Vision is that we simply "don't have the time." I beg you not to get caught in that vortex. If you don't make the time to stop and get your bearings, it is entirely possible you will end up somewhere you didn't intend.

I realize that time is at a premium these days, but there may be no better use of your limited time than to pull yourself out of the daily grind and get re-oriented to your Vision.

If you must, keep one eye focused on what you are doing. But get the other one looking up and determining where you are going. The time that it takes to do this will be the very thing that makes your future time much more effective and directed.

A DIFFERENT PERSPECTIVE

Find your life's metaphor and learn from it.

What's Your Metaphor?

One day, I went for a run. For those who know me, this is hardly noteworthy. What might surprise people about this particular run was that I really didn't want to go. It was rainy and cold, and I was alone and tired. The first part of the run was awful. I simply didn't want to be there. Every bit of my mind said, "Stop, just quit." Then the rationalizations came: "Just go tomorrow. You don't need to do this. You work hard, and you can afford to take it easy. Who are you trying to impress anyway?"

This went on until I was halfway through the run... and I realized I could make it. The second half of the run was powerful. I felt as if I had crushed a demon. That's when it hit me that, for me, running is a life metaphor. I run for health, but I also run to think. I use running to help me interpret my own life, and I learn so much from it.

This part of Reality and Hope is about your metaphor. Maybe you hate running, and that is fine. But I would encourage you to do something that provides you that kind of perspective. I have read books about people who see golf as a metaphor for life. My friend Daniel finds his metaphor in surfing. Of course, it doesn't have to be a sport — I have a client who is an avid quilter, and it is remarkable to listen to her speak with passion about what it teaches her.

I want to encourage you to find your metaphor. Perhaps you already have one, and you just haven't taken the time to see it that way.

Do something with passion and let it teach you. Learn from it. When Thoreau claimed that people live their lives in "quiet desperation," I have to think it was in part because they had no metaphor through which to learn about their own life. I hope that whatever your metaphor is, that it brings you joy. Sometimes it may also bring you pain, but in either case you can learn from it.

"Man who catch fly with chopstick accomplish anything." That one comes from Mr. Miyagi of *The Karate Kid*. Now there's a metaphor.

Musical Chairs

If you haven't heard comedian Brian Regan's bit on musical chairs, you are missing an all-time gut buster. In a nutshell, he points out that as children we play this game of musical chairs where the idea taught to 7-year olds is that there just isn't enough in life. There are not enough chairs for everyone!

As a result of this anxiety-driven little game, we end up going through our lives thinking that we must grab what we can because there's not enough and we will always be miserable. Sadly, I know too many people who, as adults, are still playing the musical chairs game — only they are playing the musical everything game and thus breeding a scarcity mindset.

As our current world turns and things are getting tighter and tighter, I implore you to recognize that scarcity and the fear of "not enough" in life can have a dangerous grip on people.

We all have a tendency now and then to focus on what we lack instead of what we have. I say let's band together and have an Abundance Revolution!

Abundance is the opposite of Scarcity. Abundance calls for us to see the world every day in terms of all that we do have — which for most of us is a lot. And I'm not just talking about material things. We have relationships and freedoms in and around us that we must recognize and keep focusing on. No amount of economic scarcity will ever take that away.

The next time you are at a 7-year old's party, I say add one more chair than the actual number of kids running in a circle. It'll be a puzzling outcome to be sure, but at least you will get to teach them all about Abundance vs. Scarcity.

Contentment

"Never be content." I remember reading this in a client's Vision document once and it stopped me in my tracks. This may seem a bit like hair splitting, but I would like you to consider the fine line between being "content" and being "complacent." There may be some who argue this point, but in general, contentment is a good thing and complacency is not.

There are times to stop, look around and simply recognize the many blessings that come our way daily. Too many people who are constantly looking to improve, won't stop to see that there is much good happening all around. Perhaps there is a fear that if they do this they will lose their edge.

When this goes unchecked for some time, the lack of contentment in business and life can end up being rather poisonous.

I believe that becoming complacent and simply accepting the status quo can lead to some terrible things as well — namely mediocrity. If this is your battle, you may need to hear some truths about what it means to fight against living a safe and unproductive life. But just as we humans do, we swing the pendulum so far one way that we simply can no longer stop and see the beauty around us or even recognize the many acts of grace and love that happen daily.

Many of us seesaw between these two concepts. I have seen the need for people to come one way or the other for their own health and growth. If, in the name of desiring to be excellent, you have a hard time stopping and recognizing there are many amazing and beautiful things happening, I recommend you courageously admit this to yourself and do something to rectify it. If you have become complacent, then you probably need to do something about that too.

It's a funny roller coaster, isn't it?

26 O'Clock

If I had a nickel for every time one of my clients wished for more hours in the day, I'd be... well, I'd be wealthy. Wishing for more hours in the day is akin to wishing for more letters in the alphabet. For those who remember the Dr. Seuss book *On Beyond Zebra*, this is exactly what the good doctor wrote about. If he were a coach in modern times, he may write a book about hours of the day that go beyond 24.

Have YOU ever wished for "more hours in the day?"

The next time you make such a wish, I invite you to consider that it isn't more hours that you need, but rather it is a deeper sense of discernment about how you spend the hours you have.

It is the ultimate form of responsibility to question your own decision making. Sometimes when we wish for something as unattainable as more hours, it is actually deflecting the responsibility, which is that we really need to iron out what we say "yes" to and what we say "no" to throughout the day.

As simple as it may sound, we just don't say "no, I can't do that right now" nearly enough. Perhaps we believe there is optimism in thinking and believing that we can do more than we should. But in the end, it will burn you.

I am becoming increasingly convinced that we can accomplish amazing things in the timeframes that we decree. When we go beyond that, all we do is begin to create pain in our life.

To continue to try and do more, and then wish for more hours, is essentially trying to find yourself living in a Dr. Seuss world. And while that may sound fun, it may not be as real as we would like.

Shower Thinkers

Not too long ago, I was fortunate enough to hear thought leader Tim Sanders speak at a sales conference. I have said many times since that I believe it was one of the most powerful talks I have ever heard. Tim spoke about many powerful concepts, and his extemporaneous style and methods were amazing.

One sort of weird thing that he asked the entire crowd was how many of us got great ideas in the shower. Over 1000 people raised their hands, almost all of whom thought they were the only ones. It was surreal.

Tim went on to explain that studies have shown that the combination of warm water and the rhythm of the spray create a 'freeing of the mind.' This freedom provides an amazing environment for broader thinking and creative brain activity. Since that very day I have gone out of my way to exploit my shower time.

Sometimes I will tell a client or friend that "I had an amazing thought in the shower this morning ... " only to be embarrassed by the fact that letting them know what I was thinking in the shower probably qualified as TMI. So if I tell you that I thought of something in the shower please don't get weird, creepy ideas!

In a recent Shower Brainstorm, I caught myself projecting the day — mind mapping, if you will. Not dissimilar to what athletes do as they project what it will look like when they are performing at a high level. I have also caught myself doing the opposite — projecting negative outcomes and playing out too many worst-case scenarios.

My hope through sharing this is to start a tribe of Shower Thinkers, and my encouragement comes in two forms:

If you are a novice shower thinker, take steps to exploit this natural brain occurrence.

If you catch yourself going negative, don't let it propagate. Awareness of this can create amazing results.

Days Like This

In 1995, the brilliant Irish singer/songwriter/poet Van Morrison released an album entitled *Days Like This*. The title track to that album is a stunning song about the fact that some days just go really well. It's a surprising tune because the euphemism alone strikes negativity. But some days are indeed filled with people who aren't complaining and opportunities that are coming to fruition; days where we don't worry and no one is in a hurry. It is a brilliant commentary on the fact that so much good actually does happen in any given day.

Now, there is an underlying assumption that there are indeed days where the opposite goes on as well. But what I cannot seem to yet understand, is why this negativity has such a strong pull on our souls. We have this obscure tendency to focus on the business deals that go astray, only to learn that they represent a small percentage of all the deals done in a given period.

I am not insinuating we shouldn't strive to have it all go well, but I am learning that Van Morrison was right — there are far more blessings around us than curses. When we get to measuring just how much of our hearts and minds are consumed by the things that impact us negatively, we need once again to be reminded that the vast majority of our life is filled with things that go well.

I want to continue to endeavor to coach myself and others to this fact. Whenever you have one of "those days," I implore you to remember that there is far more positive, good stuff happening in that day than the one or two things that may take you out.

Beware

I titled this page "beware" partly because it has a bit of a hook. "Beware" can capture our eye, getting us concerned and thinking, "beware of what?" What has really been on my heart and coming through in my coaching isn't the idea of scarcity and how we should "beware" of some situation or circumstance, but rather that we could all take steps to "be aware." Steps that would allow us to be aware of what we are feeling and thinking as we continue to navigate through these tumultuous times.

We can write and speak about the spirit of fear and scarcity until we're blue, but we must keep "being aware" of its effects on our own life as well as the effects of it in our vocations. I don't think I have ever coached anyone who hasn't suffered from some form of fear and scarcity.

Almost every one of us wishes there were some "magic pill" cure for conquering our own little fears — and I wish I had a one-size fits all answer to give you. What I can say, is that being aware of how you are feeling — a true awareness of how your emotions are impacting your actions and the people around you — can be a huge piece of your own solution.

So be aware. Be aware this week of situations and circumstances that make your blood boil or that cause you great grief. Be aware also of situations that cause you to feel joy and relief.

This isn't the whole solution to conquering fears, but the awareness we have can take us all quite a ways.

What Does it Cost?

Thomas Jefferson was an interesting character. He was arguably the most influential person in the writing of the Declaration of Independence, and later served as our third president. He was an archaeologist, horticulturist, paleontologist, and architect. He built and founded the University of Virginia.

President Kennedy once remarked to 49 Nobel Prize winners who he had invited to the White House that "I think this is the most extraordinary collection of talent, of human knowledge, that has ever been gathered together at the White House — with the possible exception of when Thomas Jefferson dined alone."

OK, enough of the history lesson, you get the point — he was really smart. Jefferson is credited with many well-known sayings, but one that strikes me every time I hear it is this: "How much pain have cost us the evils which have never happened." This is 18th century lingo for "Gosh, we worry about a ton of stuff that never even happens."

Too often we live our lives with so much needless worry. Now, that doesn't mean that from time to time real things don't happen. It simply means that we should pay attention to what occupies our mind and our hearts, and realize that most of our concerns will never come about.

It is possible that if we fret too much, our very fretting and festering can create a self-fulfilling prophecy. If we sit around long enough worrying about the potential consequences of action, then we never actually take action. Then we give ourselves justification for the worry, and the wheels on the bus go round and round.

A colleague of mine recently told me that her mom had the daunting task of facing chemotherapy, and she was concerned about the possible side effects. The attending oncologist wisely suggested that the good woman go about her life, without waiting around for symptoms which she may never experience anyway.

We could all stand to learn this valuable lesson.

Ah... The Good Ol' Days

Take a second and remember a time in your life when you were peaceful, happy, and carefree. Was it in your college years? Was it when you were a young kid playing in your backyard? Do you remember a vacation or Christmas that was especially pleasant? Did your job used to offer you something much better and easier?

These collective memories are what we call "The Good Ol' Days." I suppose it is normal and even healthy to have positive memories. But, like almost any good thing in life, we have a strange propensity to overdo it. We take something that is good and exaggerate it, diminish it, distort it, or twist it until we make it bad.

I have encountered many people facing tough times who desperately want to hold on to the past. Frankly, this is a normal reaction, but it isn't always healthy. Remembering past days, past actions, and things that we used to be able to do may keep us from finding contentment in the present.

I have written about the power of embracing who and where we are. Still I find that many of us keep looking back and dreaming about days gone by. I understand that this can give us some repose from our current realities, but it can also become an unintentional avoidance of living in the here and now.

Almost every major religion or philosophy in the world espouses some form of living in the present. We can definitely learn from this over and over again. Embracing today for all it has to offer, both the good and the bad, will be a lifelong challenge. We simply must accept that there are some things we can no longer do, and roads that are closed to us.

The good news is that there are always new roads to take and new frontiers to cross. Embrace the present and dedicate yourself to excellence in the small things today. In so doing, you will effectively create a future that is full of new happy memories.

May your "good ol' days" be your fuel, rather than a ball and chain.

The Power to Choose

Over the years, there have been some pretty crazy happenings in the lives of my clients — and by "crazy," I do not always mean good crazy. It is so easy to allow our minds to go to the negative. We allow the very real, but all too dark aspects of life to infiltrate our thoughts and cause our entire worldview to go black.

If I were to ask you to sit right now and make a list of all the things that tick you off or upset you, most of you would quickly come up with an extensive list.

On a particularly frustrating day, I was mentally creating a list of my own when it hit me that making lists of annoyances and grievances in my head was my choice. And if I could choose to do that, then I am equally free to make a different choice.

I can make a list of my blessings. When "stuff" in this world happens to us, we allow it to sink in and we make a choice about what to do with it. It is a choice. Let me repeat: it is a choice.

I repeat that for my own sake because it is simply remarkable how, after all these years, I still pretend that my thoughts are beyond my control. Upon reflection, I am reminded that I get to choose a different path in my mind. It's funny how we all need that reminder over and over.

You cannot control all that happens to you today, but you do have amazing control over what you do in your mind and heart with what happens. My hope is that this doesn't sound too squishy. Choose wisely.

Beat the BTDTs

We live in a world where some of the most amazing technology becomes obsolete before many of us even know what it is. In some respects, our rapid advances are remarkable, but in other ways we are learning to be bored by things that aren't new and flashy. Just as quickly as we lose interest in new technology, we can become bored with some of the simple things in our business and our lives. We desire to move to flashier things before we have mastered the necessary basics.

Our incessant need for newness can create an environment in which we suffer from what I call the BTDT's — "Been There, Done That."

Do you measure the little things in your business? Are you taking time to review your plans? Are you adhering to a time block? Have you read your life plan lately? These are just some simple examples of tactics and strategies that we learned, but have abandoned in the pursuit of something new.

Now, I am all for a fresh coat of paint, and I believe that there are some wonderful new ideas and strategies out there. But I am a firm believer that almost all of us have a few critical components of our business and our life that we need to get back to.

For example, have you ever re-read a book that was meaningful to you years ago? I recently re-scanned John Maxwell's *21 Irrefutable Laws of Leadership*, and was re-ignited by some of the Laws that I had forgotten. I am certainly not implying that you need to live in antiquity or shy away from all things new. I am, however, warning that you may inadvertently get the BTDT's because of how fast the world turns.

There are probably some old, seemingly stale things that you need to dust off and revitalize. Try it. You may find that the disciplines, actions, and principles that once brought you success are still there, waiting to serve you all over again.

Saving Coins

My son and I have an ongoing debate about the nature of our feelings and emotions. When something bad comes to pass, he believes that you simply cannot control how you feel about it. I try to explain, with all my feeble fatherly wisdom, that one does indeed have control over how they choose to respond to a situation. Our debate can sometimes get quite contentious. How ironic that a debate over our emotional control can cause both of us to feel bad. I think I get particularly fired up about this because there is something in my soul that knows exactly what he is talking about. There are times when I get assaulted, even hijacked, by my own response to situations. I have noticed this also happens to many of the people I coach. In fact, I dare say that this emotional attack happens to everyone. Some, however, have learned how to escape from it quicker than others.

There are many strategies that people use to return to a place of wholeness and peace in those situations. I just want to offer one: If you find yourself caught in a moment of grief, it is healthy to realize that how you feel is not wrong, but rather it is only one side of a coin.

The flip side of that coin is that there are some really great situations, people, and circumstances around you. It is possible to choose to see that side of the coin, even in moments of struggle. So there is my simple strategy — think of a coin. In fact, you may even keep a special one with you for just such an occasion.

By choosing to see both sides of our circumstances, we can gently move away from the idea that all is bad and only the dark side is real. It never is. This simple practice can pull you out of a negative spiral. Then, when we are freed from that prison, we can get back to helping others see both sides of their own coins.

Your Personal Tag Cloud

I get to learn something new every day. Recently, I learned what a "Tag Cloud" is. A Tag Cloud is a collection of key words that are brought together from a larger body of work and smashed into a single work of art. A colleague of mine created a Tag Cloud on a site called Wordle (www.wordle.net) of every blog post I had written for two years. It was an odd feeling to look at this conglomerate of thoughts and realize that these were the most frequently used words in my writing. Wordle increases the size of the word based on frequency of use. So in my Tag Cloud, I could clearly see that I write often about "People" and "Time," and less often about "Foil" and "Trout." At a quick glance, I thought it fair to say that my blog is very much about positive things, and also things like the "Enemy." There were also words like "Surround" and "Emotions" and "Courage." Not only is this a cool way to view a body of knowledge, but it also got me thinking about what my personal Tag Cloud would look like.

Imagine a visual representation of all that is going on in your head every day. What words would be in your picture? Would your personal cloud be more positive or negative? What would it say about the condition of your heart? If it were possible to view and study the words that are within you, would you be proud of them?

Self awareness is crucial to our growth. Being aware of your internal language can illuminate the difference between what you think about all day long and who you want to become as a person. Is there a gap? Take a look at a Tag Cloud, and then consider what yours would include if it were possible to splash it up on a screen. Over time, your actions and the path of your very life will come to reflect these words.

May your personal cloud have a silver lining!

What's New

There are many different ideas out there about how to become and stay successful in any given endeavor. One ingredient that I have consistently seen in the best is their willingness to re-create themselves, to bring something daring and new to their job, their team, or their clients.

It is stunning how so many people get trapped in their own ruts. They stubbornly refuse the simple time-tested strategies that will allow them to see their jobs in a new way.

If you believe that bringing a fresh perspective to your job is important, I want to encourage you to consider two simple things that could help you break through the mundane nature of your job.

1. Recognize that stress is the enemy of innovation and creation.

In addition to the many detrimental things that doctors say can happen to our physical bodies when we are overly stressed, an underlying by-product is that we lack the mental space needed to create.

I understand that it is not helpful to just say, "don't be stressed." Do you need to take some time away? Do you need to meet with a friend or colleague about it? When we unwind from the pressures of our lives, we are free to see things in a new way and discover new paths.

2. Be intentional about creativity.

Getting out of your normal environment can be the push you need to see an old problem in a new way. You can go somewhere as close as the local coffee house or as far as a plane ride to a great new locale. And then, invite someone else. Too often we think we can create by ourselves. You may be shocked to learn that you simply don't have all of the answers. Odds are, whoever you invite could stand to have help with their creativity as well.

Let's go get new — our future may depend on it!

Organized or Paralyzed?

"I need to get organized!" If you naturally tend toward living an organized life, then feel free to ignore this page. For the rest of us, we need to take heed. Having a disorganized environment could be holding you back today. It could be your desk, your office, your car, your finances, or some other aspect of your business or life that is in disarray.

When we fail to address the clutter of our environment, it begins to permeate all aspects of our lives and eventually impacts how we think and feel.

This problem is especially poignant for people with dominant behavioral styles and highly relational behavioral styles. (For those who are familiar with DISC, I am talking about "High D" and "High I.") Dominant people are often big picture thinkers who don't like the minutia and the detail aspect of organization. Relational folks simply don't see things in patterns, and thus they find themselves living in a chaotic environment.

Fortunately, if you recognize one of these behavioral styles in yourself, there is something you can do.

Set aside a specific time when you will do nothing but organize and straighten your environment. Schedule this time as you would an important meeting. Simply stating "I need to get organized" will not help you. Most people think about getting organized, and many even talk about it frequently, but few actually schedule the time to make it happen.

The great irony is that, even as we think we are too busy to spend time on organization, the busyness we feel is a by-product of our disorganization. Let's get off that hamster wheel and make a date with ourselves to organize our environment.

A fresh start could be the very wind our sails need right now.

Changes

I cannot remember a season with as much change as this one. In times like these, it can seem like life is swirling out of control. And it seems inevitable that change will keep coming. What I wish to call to the forefront of our minds is that we can do very little, if anything, to thwart change. What we absolutely can do is to be aware of our response to it.

I see people around me lamenting the changes, to the point of stifling their own growth. I want to say this in the clearest way that I know how: Your response to the changes around you is either going to be a competitive advantage or disadvantage. You get to choose.

We live in a free country — God bless the USA. But with that freedom comes the ability to choose your reaction to everything that comes your way. If you choose to argue, despise, complain, fight, or rally against inevitable change, you must know that you are expressing a freedom to do so.

No one plans to lose a job or have difficult family situations arise. However, it is this very freedom to respond to these situations that can either bring us clarity or trap us in a self-made prison.

You do not have to fake your feelings and pretend that you love all of the changes. But responding positively to change is nothing shy of an advantage over all of those who don't. Please, do not underestimate the power of your response. Choose to make it a great day!

What Can You Lose?

"Train yourself to let go of everything you fear to lose." This quote about the fear of losing things is timely, relevant, and on the money. Fascinatingly, it was uttered by none other than Yoda, the Jedi master. We can all learn from the backward-speaking little green guy.

Fear is an ever-present force in our world. As we continue through this current economic and vocational reality, fear is an increasingly popular emotion. Many of us fear losing our jobs, losing our clients, losing our possessions. The fear of loss is a debilitating problem. Among other things, it can lead to scarcity and greed. We must, as Yoda puts it, "train ourselves" to let go. Holding onto things too tightly can be the very catalyst for the loss of them. That may sound like twisted and complicated logic, but to hold things with an open hand will make you a freer person who has an increasing ability to inspire others.

It is a dangerous irony that the less we perceive we have, the tighter we hold it. The tighter we hold, the less we can give. And the less we give, the less we will have. After I wrote that last paragraph, I had to go back and read it a few times to make sure I grasped it. I feel that it is true, and I also know that we can all do better at holding loosely.

Living in fear is spirit sucking. We all have some fear, but as times get tougher fear is on the rise. When we fear loss, we create a downward spiral that can end up being a bit of a self-fulfilling prophecy. I don't mean to dole out action plans, but if you or someone close to you is suffering with the dreaded fear of loss, call it out. Talk about it, and then begin training yourself to let it go.

After all, "freedom is just another word for 'nothing left to lose.'" Those words were penned by Kris Kristofferson and made famous by Janis Joplin.

Ah, the wonderful people we can learn from!

Perspective

My family and I traveled to war-torn Tijuana recently, and once again, we were able to see first-hand how much of the world lives. I do not necessarily recommend you take your family over the border in order to have perspective on this. But I am still stunned at just how blessed we are as a nation.

Yes, I do understand that unemployment is up and that for many people these times are particularly difficult. But if we could only have the eyes to see how much of humanity lives day in and day out, I am convinced that we would have a different daily perspective. Paul Simon wrote a song entitled "Born at the Right Time," and in that song he sings this: "never been lonely, never been lied to, never had to scuffle in fear, nothing denied to…" I assure you that most of us don't have complete perspective on what it means to be alone and without hope, or what it means to live in fear and squalor.

We have the perspective we do based upon the reality in which we live. Sometimes when you are able to experience someone else's reality, it can bring you a different perspective. Today, I am choosing to be grateful for what I have been given rather than focus on the list of things I may not have. If you are reading this, I assure you that you have within you a number of things to be grateful for. Make sure that you get that gratitude list out in front of you, so you do not lose sight of these things.

Today you have a choice about what you will focus on — that's the beauty (and danger) of free will. Choose gratitude. If you do, your ability to impact the world for good will increase exponentially. As you may have noticed, I coach people a great deal about gratitude and positions of the heart. I am coming to understand just how often I need to be reminded.

REFRESH YOUR SPIRIT

Stop. Break away. Put down all of your electronic devices and go and think for a few hours.

A Sound Purpose

If you don't know why, you may not even try.

I am amazed at just how important it is to remember why you do what you do. If you don't keep your big "why" on your mind and tucked into your heart, all sorts of crazy things can happen — and few of them are good.

There is an underlying current in our country that can best be described as a lack of passion. There are scores of people who are reporting that they feel little enthusiasm for their vocations. Now, I do not believe that we should expect to love what we do every single minute of every day. That just isn't realistic. However, the other extreme is that we've become indifferent, even pessimistic about what we are doing with our lives.

Success in your vocation (irrespective of how you define "success") may depend on your willingness to unearth your "why."

I, and the many great coaches I have worked with, have coached thousands of people to discover and live out their core purpose. Interestingly enough, the discovery itself often requires the kind of passion you don't feel like you have. There are only a couple of actions that I would shove down someone's throat, and one of them is to fight through any blocks you may have to discover your core purpose.

There are amazing and unexpected benefits of knowing deeply who you are and why you do what you do. If you are waking up day after day and floating through the world without a compelling purpose, it is only a matter of time before your success begins to run dry. The good news is that your purpose is already there, awaiting your discovery and nurturing.

If you are reading this and convincing yourself that you haven't the time (or even the desire) to go and discover your purpose, then I beg you to see that you are a key part of what is causing your own life to stall. Those who wrestle for their purpose are rewarded in countless ways.

A heartfelt purpose will pull you through any challenging time.

Brevity

I don't mean to get overly philosophical, but it's true that the older one gets, the more quickly time seems to pass. No wonder some of the greatest thinkers of the ages referred to life as a "mist" and a "vapor," or like grass that sprouts in the morning and is withered by evening.

I don't believe these concepts were intended to depress us. Rather, they were meant to cause us to be that much more aware of how precious time is and how important it is that we do all we can with what we have. No one escapes this life without pain — there's the "reality" piece of Reality and Hope. But have you ever noticed that there are times when tough events occur and it makes you that much more aware of and grateful for the things you have?

Why can't we practice that gratitude without the stark reminder of the pain? I long to get better at that.

Have you ever noticed that you are thankful for your health when someone around you has lost theirs or even when you are recently recovered from some pain or discomfort yourself? Perhaps the best possible thing we can do is carry that gratitude and perspective with us at all times.

I do believe that it is honorable to draw closer to your friends and family in times of need and to overtly recognize that what you have is precious and should be cherished always. I propose that you take a few minutes today and count your blessings. If there is hurt, whether it is physical or emotional, then do all you can to comfort and care for people, irrespective of your own situation.

Life is brief and the best way I know to make the most of it is to love and care for others. "Greater love has no one than this: to lay down one's life for one's friends." John 15:13

The Best Approach

Memorial Day, Veterans Day, and the Fourth of July bring out all types of well-wishes to our military, and that is a wonderful thing.

We should absolutely be grateful. But the truth is that we should be grateful every day, not just once or twice a year. I thank every man and woman I see in a military uniform, and I will continue that practice indefinitely. There is nothing like looking into the eyes of someone who has chosen to sacrifice their time and their life for our country, and thanking them. Let us never tire of doing this — they need and deserve our gratitude.

Beyond the thanks that we can give these men and women, we can all learn again the power of gratitude in our own lives. To wake up and work with a thankful heart is to make a huge difference in the world. Thankfulness and gratitude are woefully lacking in our country. The good Lord knows that there are many realities that can cause us to develop a cynical, skeptical, darkened heart. But this will only lead us down a dead end road. You may be completely right about all of your lamentations, but a soured heart will take its toll on you in so many ways that it would be impossible to name them all.

Today, practice the art of thankfulness and gratitude. I believe it is something that one can develop and get better at through practice. The world will throw all kinds of reasons at us to be the opposite. We must fight against this, and be intentionally grateful for the many blessings we do have.

When you practice gratitude more and more, you will find that you are not only much more attractive to others, but you are also more open to learning. Gratitude begets more gratitude. Should you choose to practice this today, and again tomorrow, you will soon find yourself in an upward spiral. This is actually a very simple practice. Don't overthink it. Just do it.

There is no holiday, season, or day that goes by in which having a grateful heart will not help you.

Starting All Over Again

I coach many people who are sick and tired of starting over. I must admit that from time to time it fatigues me, too. However, we need to embrace the idea. If we don't, we are in danger of getting beaten down, beleaguered and burned out. If you think about it, life is a series of restarts. This is precisely why King Solomon claimed that "there is nothing new under the sun." (Ecclesiastes 1:9)

When you hear those words, you could decide that you are doomed to live a life of meaningless repetition. Or, you could take it as a challenge to see the same old things with new eyes.

What do you need to see for the first time, again? You could look at this week as just another week, seven days like any other. Or, you could choose to see it as an opportunity to begin again and build something fantastic. This is precisely the posture that one needs to sustain long-term success.

Do you need to go back to some old relationships and re-spark them? Do you need to meet with your team and create some new challenges for this quarter? Do you need to re-commit yourself to a discipline that has fallen by the wayside? This is great time to do so.

We are constantly re-making ourselves. Some people choose to exploit this, while others choose to get frustrated. You can imagine which path I am in favor of.

So what's it going to be? I will end with another idea from good ol' King Sol: "There is a time for everything, and a season for every activity under the heavens." (Ecclesiastes 3:1) Now could be your season to start something over.

Embrace it for what it is, and make this next season great.

Throwing in the Towel

In tough times, I hear many people declare that they want to give up. It got my mind spinning around the idea of "throwing in the towel." I can only assume that the term originated in boxing, when a trainer would stop a fight because his poor student was getting bludgeoned in the ring. It was a way to declare defeat before the poor guy dropped for good.

If you feel like you are getting beat up right now, and you're thinking about throwing in the towel... don't. At least, not yet. Now, there are circumstances in which this could be the wise thing to do. If you are on the brink of emotional, physical, or mental breakdown, you should at least take a time out. More often than not, when we want to give up, all we really need is to step back from our circumstances and reflect. There have been times when I have seen key decisions made by someone who refused to return to their corner. Do not react. Have the courage and mental acuity to realize what you are doing and force yourself into some reflection. Step back from the situation and come back at it when you have greater clarity and peace. If indeed you need to throw in the towel, do so only after deep reflection, clear counsel, and good old-fashioned time. Burnout is an issue in times of change, and towel-throwing is talked about a lot. Making the right decision to quit requires you to be at your best. Are you really at your best when you are in the very circumstance that is causing you to spin?

Stop. Break away. Put down all of your electronic devices and go and think for a few hours. To do so could not only save your career, but also save you from making a decision that could change your circumstances for the worse. I am all for hard work, but not to the point where we can put ourselves in a position to throw in towels prematurely. It is very likely that this action could create wonderful things for your future.

Off Time

The topic of "Time Management" has been beaten to death. There are countless resources claiming to teach you to prioritize and "manage" your time. All week long, I coach people on living a disciplined life. I define discipline as the act of doing what you should, when you should, whether you feel like it or not. But in our quest to be disciplined and productive with every moment, we rarely schedule "off time" anymore — time to relax and just be in the moment.

Sometimes we can still find this time on vacations, but for most of us these do not come frequently enough. There is a real need to find even short bits of relief every day. The question I have is this — do you intentionally schedule "off time"? Can you allow yourself to unplug from the frenetic world and just BE, if only for a few moments every day?

I find this time when I run. Ironically, for me running is like being still — although my body is in motion, my mind can breathe.

What do you do to unplug and be still? Do you walk? Do you read? Do you crochet? Do you listen to music? Do you pray or meditate? Any of these activities can be good ways to unplug from our fast-paced lives every now and then. Whenever we go through seasons when we don't seek out this time, we get carried away by the urgencies around us. Some daily "off time" from the world will help you come back in with a refreshed perspective.

Just remember that you may have to schedule this time intentionally, because it doesn't seem to come naturally any more.

Against the Wind

What is it about the human heart that makes negativity so attractive?

Have you read the news lately? Spare yourself. I realize that many people will have their own personal theories about this, but I am stunned about just how negative the news and media at large is.

I don't doubt that there are some awful things going on in our country and throughout the world. Unemployment, people killing each other, political and personal scandals, despair and strife all around us… this is what you will get if you turn on the news. The weird thing is that they probably wouldn't feed it to us if we didn't have an appetite for it.

Now, it isn't that I am a proponent of turning a blind eye to reality. But if we are to live a higher order and become the people that we were designed to become, we must lean against this pervasive wind of negativity.

There are many awful byproducts of ingesting this antipathy, but perhaps the most toxic is that when we do, we simply cannot care for others at the level we need to. Think about it — if your vocation is in some way about helping or leading others (and that includes just about everyone!) how can you excel if your mind and heart are weighed down with the worries and dissensions of life day in and day out?

Let us always remember that, while many of these realities exist, we need not allow them to infiltrate our beings. Keep some inner peace and take pleasure in the small positive details in life. In this way we will be fully equipped to serve the world.

Prepare for Peace

Peace. That intangible sense that all is well and things are in order.

In all of my coaching, I would say that this is probably the single most sought-after characteristic of our lives. Many people pursue possessions, success, money… but even the most materialistic Grinch really just wants peace. The truth is, we can choose to have peace in our lives. But most people don't believe that. They have given in to the demands of the world to the extent that peace seems like a far-off wish. If I could offer up a simple and sincere prayer, it would be that you find peace. Even if it is for one day, choose it. There will be many days ahead filled with strivings and accomplishments, plans and successes. Today, I invite you to do something radical. Disengage with everything the world around you says is a "must do," and simply be present with the closest people to you.

Play cards, play games, watch a favorite movie with your family, or read a great book. Drink some tea in the afternoon and talk eye-to-eye with an aging family member or a good friend. Slow down enough to let the pressures of life slip away as you choose peace. May we all find the very joy that our strivings are all about.

Challenges Yet to Come

I would guess that we all know people who have battled through a horrific illness. In the midst of such a time, it is easy to remember days where your own health was taken for granted. I work with people who are going through tremendous relational or marital issues. As they navigate the difficulty, it is easy to remember a time when relationships were healthy — and then long for them to be restored.

Often it takes a catastrophic event to remind us about how we shouldn't have taken our health, our relationships, or our prosperity for granted. This is yet another great argument on behalf of completing a plan for your life.

A life plan isn't just a matter of taking account of the key challenges in life; it can be just as powerful in protecting the areas in your life that are doing well.

I have to admit that I myself am not as grateful as I should be for my health and relationships, my job and my friendships. I am reminded of the fact that people lose these things every day. I am going to once again recommit myself to my life's plan. I will not only focus on the key areas for improvement, but also on the areas that are doing well — so as to never take them for granted. I implore you to join me in this activity.

As Psalm 118:24 implores, "let us rejoice today and be glad." What key aspect of your life should you protect? Let us collectively make an effort to sharpen the areas of our lives that are going well.

Ramparts, Really?

The next time you hear the "Star Spangled Banner," I implore you to contemplate the words. We hear this anthem at sporting events, and certainly during the Olympics. Sometimes we are moved to tears just listening to the familiar tune, watching as our fellow Americans reverently honor this land of the free. Few people take the time to consider that this song is actually a poem about personal and communal sacrifice. How great would it be if more of us considered the acts of sacrifice that had to be made "through the night" while bombs burst in the air to protect our flag and our freedom?

I'm not necessarily trying to make a point about patriotism here, though I think that is a fine and noble characteristic. Instead, my hope is that we could all do some translation and interpretation into our own worlds. What do we sacrifice? What comforts are we willing to forgo for a greater purpose?

How fascinating it is that we are so emotionally drawn in when we witness an athlete standing under our flag listening to that anthem about sacrifice, even as the athlete undoubtedly made tremendous sacrifices in their own life to make it onto that very platform.

Now, it is very likely that none of us will ever win a gold medal in the Olympics, and perhaps we won't even win any congressional medals for patriotism or bravery. But I propose that each of us can embrace the idea of sacrifice at a deeper level. Furthermore, it is my hope and my prayer that when we hear our nation's great anthem, we will take it as a reminder to be great in our own lives.

A Time for Everything

I have often made reference to King Solomon's wise words about seasons. In Ecclesiastes 3, he writes that there is a time for everything: "a time to be born and a time to die, a time to plant and a time to uproot, a time to kill and a time to heal."

I am drawn to the idea of seasons because it so accurately represents Reality and Hope. If I were to focus on reality all the time, I may as well ask you to go and read the *New York Times* every day. That's enough reality to choke an elephant. The news so rarely provides us much hope.

I still marvel at the way our culture feeds on negativity. Is it because if we see enough bad stuff, it will somehow make us feel better about ourselves?

For the moment, I am going to camp squarely on hope. As I hunted for hope, I came across the following words: "Hope deferred makes the heart sick, but a longing fulfilled is a tree of life." (Proverbs 13:12)

I suppose one could view the whole concept of "living your dreams" as a bit fluffy, but the truth is that there is something deep and meaningful about longing for better things in the future. When we don't, our hearts are literally sick. Let today be about your dreams. If it has been a while since you have allowed yourself to go there, GO! Dream, plan, and envision something great. Don't defer.

Never forget that hopes and dreams are "trees of life."

Above All Else

There is a well-known proverb, from the actual book of Proverbs, that states "Above all else, guard your heart, for everything you do flows from it." I have been particularly keen on finding those areas that take pieces of our heart in a way that causes us to have a less full and fruitful life. Perhaps it is a specific relationship. Maybe it is a certain situation. Or maybe it is even a personal behavior you do repeatedly, which causes your heart to be less than "guarded."

So what does it look like for you to guard your heart? In order to answer that question you may need to figure out where and how your heart gets stomped on. Sadly, I know too many people who do the stomping themselves. They stubbornly choose to assault their own hearts through negative self talk and projecting and planning negative outcomes. For some crazy reason, this seems to be all too common.

The wise King Solomon heralded that ABOVE ALL ELSE we need to be on guard for those things that assault us at the deepest level. It is only when our hearts are whole that we can build great things in the world.

It is easy to get inadvertently mired down in situations and circumstances that cause damage to our hearts. Let us rise above this and play with a whole heart.

The Finish Line

The pace at which most of us run these days is quite staggering. And yet, most every person I coach longs to have more time to reflect. It is amazing, if not humorously ironic, that taking time to reflect on our lives and our businesses is most needed when we have the least time for it. Ah… to be too busy to do the kind of reflection that would be a catalyst for making the changes necessary to get you out of the busyness trap.

I ask that you take intentional time to reflect. The end of the year can provide a great setting for this kind of reflection, but you needn't wait to receive the benefits it can bring. What have you learned lately? What sort of challenges did you face? What did these challenges teach you? What opportunities did you capitalize on and which did you miss? Where were the rough spots and how did you respond to them?

Regardless of the time of the year, it is wise to reflect upon (and write down) what you are thankful for.

After this kind of reflection, it is good to then look forward and make a plan for next year. Some will have more elaborate plans than others, but no one is immune to the benefit of having a plan. My coaching to you is to be intentional about a day of reflection and planning. Our busy world screams that slowing down and doing such reflection is nothing more than a waste of precious time. Do not buy this lie.

Be strong, be intentional, reflect and make a plan.

COURAGEOUS PERSISTENCE

There is a reservoir there that can allow you to go further and do more for people than any of us can possibly imagine.

Keep Going

While on a run recently, I noticed a sign that said "No Loitering." As I read those words, I began to consider whether loitering is ever a good idea. The verb "to loiter" means "to stand around idly or without apparent purpose." At times, I have caught the people I coach doing some professional loitering.

Winston Churchill once said, "If you are going through hell, keep going." In other words, don't loiter — especially in your most hellish places.

Sometimes we loiter because we are paralyzed by our own thoughts. We obsess over questions like, "What is going to happen tomorrow?" or "Why didn't I do that sooner?" or "Did I make the right decision?" When we mentally stop to consider these questions, we can sometimes get caught loitering. We cause our own paralysis because we take too long to answer the question.

Whether or not you find satisfying answers to your questions, the next step is always the same — take a next step. Stop loitering.

I am all for reflection, for seeking a better understanding of why we do what we do. But I find that people linger far too long in the How and Why and What If, and it is leading to inaction. If you are feeling paralyzed by future outcomes or past decisions, the best thing you can do is heed Mr. Churchill's advice, and KEEP GOING! It is possibly the greatest thing you can do for your business.

Remember that some of the best next steps aren't always the biggest. Even small steps are enough to keep us going in the right direction.

Getting Gritty

Do you know of someone you would characterize as a person with grit? Grit is a quality we all need.

If you say the word "grit" over and over, it starts to sound goofy. If you are in the Southern part of our country, perhaps you had grits for breakfast. But that isn't what we are talking about here.

Having grit means possessing an indomitable spirit. When you have grit, you are not easily swayed by tough times and rattling situations. You look into the face of challenges, and see them as just one more thing to be stared down and beaten.

We need more people to possess this trait in our world right now.

There is an endless supply of reasons to be beaten down these days. There are relational reasons and economic reasons, vocational reasons and health reasons. You could probably stop right now and make a robust list of all the things in your life that have the ability to tank you and get your spirit sideways. In fact, your list may include items that are beyond your control, and even things that you are absolutely right about. But being a person of grit means taking on all of these real challenges and thriving, day in and day out, just because you can.

One of the most commonly travelled roads is one filled with people who have every reason to be down. The road that fewer are on is one where high-character individuals are doing great things and helping as many people as they can, irrespective of their circumstances.

In the end, though difficult, I believe that grit is a learnable, developable trait. I have this suspicion we are going to need more of it in the coming days.

Grit Happens!

The Better You Become…

I coach some very dialed-in executives, salespeople, and leaders. I am blessed to be surrounded by some very good and thoughtful people, from whom I can learn so much. One consistent challenge I have with this group of people is when I assume that they have their business and their lives pretty much figured out. This can cause me to inadvertently neglect asking important questions and challenging assumptions.

If you are in a season where things are going quite well, I encourage you to never stop asking questions, especially the most basic questions about who you are and what you do. You may already be familiar with the learning model, first conceived by Abraham Maslow, whereby one goes through these four stages:

Unconscious Incompetence: You don't know that you don't know

Conscious Incompetence: You become aware that there is something you don't know

Conscious Competence: Now you know, but have to work to remain aware of your "knowing"

Unconscious Competence: You know it so well that it no longer is part of your conscious thought. I used to conclude that we all need to get to the ideal of Stage 4, like a world-class athlete who is so skilled they no longer need to consider the fundamentals — they just perform.

The best of the best can get to that final stage, but "unconscious competence" can turn back into incompetence if you're not paying attention. In many ways, Stage 3 — Conscious Competence — is the better stage for our vocations. To remain conscious is to keep asking questions and not take for granted that we all need to review and adhere to the basics over and over again.

One key way to do this is to allow your coach, friend, colleague, or someone close to you to ask basic questions without feeling offended. It may be those very basics that we slip away from "unconsciously." Never get so good that you don't keep challenging the premise of your own success. Better to stay alert and aware.

Start Over

I have experienced a phenomenon in my coaching. Many of my clients begin a new discipline or shoot for some new goal, only to miss the mark or not attain the level of discipline they were aiming at. When this happens, the vast majority of people throw in the proverbial towel. In the quiet of their own heart, they simply stop trying. They reason that the most surefire way to not fail is to stop attempting.

The wisest of people I know do the opposite. They shamelessly and willfully step back up to the plate and take another swing.

I believe it was Wayne Gretsky who said, "You miss 100% of the shots you don't take." It takes a certain amount of courage to keep shooting, even when you miss the mark. Wherever you find yourself in these precarious times, those who will survive and thrive will not be the wisest of us, but rather those who keep trying every day. If you miss your goal or if you fall short of your own disciplines, I implore you to muster the courage and start again. And again. And again.

Reminders are Everywhere

Some time ago, I attended my son's 8th grade graduation. As part of the festivities, each graduate gave a "speech." These talks ranged from written down words on a 3x5 card to memorized poems and anecdotes.

Most of the kids, as you can imagine, ranged anywhere from fairly nervous to scared out of their minds. One of the boys, Joshua, stood up to speak and was obviously rattled. Josh stammered, stuttered, and quite literally shook in fear. At one point this young man actually had an outbreak of what looked like anger or frustration at his own inability to continue his talk.

Imagine this 14-year old boy in front of his classmates, teachers and all of the parents. There were long pauses, frustrated tears, and a few words. All of this would have been more than a little vexing if it weren't for the fact that Josh has autism. Everyone knew how hard he was trying. No one helped him because he had told the teachers he wanted to do this by himself.

When he finished, everyone broke into a huge applause.

I was left standing there with a picture of courage that humbled me. It made me realize that there are subtle actions and simple gestures all around us that can inspire us to do better. Reach into your heart today. Remember that there is a reservoir there that can allow you to go further and do more for people than any of us can possibly imagine! May fear cower under the weight of your heart's desire to impact the world.

Possibilities in Uncertain Times

"Maturity of mind is the capacity to endure uncertainty." This quote by John Finey encapsulates a very intriguing, if not necessary, principle for so many of us. If we are to "endure" then we must embrace uncertainty. If you were to go out today and interview 50 prominent, respectable economists and ask what they believe is going to happen to our country in the next 12 months, you would get 50 different answers. There would probably be some congruencies, but since many of these people get paid to give their opinion, none would consider "I don't know" to be a very good answer.

But really, it seems like the best answer: "We don't know."

Since I don't get paid to offer an opinion, let me be one of the few to offer this prediction — we're not sure, so we must embrace uncertainty.

Embracing it means that you would go out today, in your given vocation, and you would be great notwithstanding the fact that you don't know what tomorrow holds. The funny thing is that even if we did know, would our actions change? I have found that *Reality and Hope* is in so many ways written to encourage people to go forth and do what they should, when they should, whether or not they feel like it. That means taking action in your particular moment of time, whether or not you have a pulse on what the future holds.

It is not bad to consider the possibilities of the future and it is certainly okay to make plans and have contingencies, but too many of us are hemmed up by not knowing. It is actually quite remarkable that we can accomplish so much without really needing to know all that the future holds.

To "endure" means to last, to persevere. To do so in uncertain times — and not get choked by the unknown — is a test of your character. Go make today great and let tomorrow be about tomorrow.

Thankful for my Horse

There is an old adage that states "you must get back on the horse that threw you." The idiom implies that we have attempted to do something (like create a new habit or shoot for a big goal) and failed. Sometimes the failure is more frequent than any of us would be comfortable to admit. I have noticed that it takes a great deal of courage to get back on a horse after repeated failure. If we are to become the people we were created to be however, we must continue to get up and we must keep getting back on our horse.

Sometimes I get sick of having to get up and back on my horse — but I am grateful that he is still around!

I have found that when people get knocked off a horse once, or perhaps a few times, they prefer to simply stay on the ground. There is an element of humility that comes into play about getting up and getting back on your horse.

We sometimes think that if we stop trying to get back on, then there is no way we can get bucked off again. Repeated failure is a common fear, but if we don't conquer that fear then we will simply be choosing to stay on the ground. It may feel safe down there, but it is and will always be the ground.

So what habit must you get back on? What discipline has bucked you off a few times that you simply need to attack again? Is it a commitment to your health? Is it a specific, tangible action you must take in your work? There is no shame in reclaiming an old commitment regardless of how many tries and fails you've had. But there is potential regret in not getting back up and recommitting. Horses are large, powerful animals, but they are also patient and willing toward those who stand ready to re-commit.

Never fear what others may say or think about your re-commitments. Remember that the horse could care less.

Get back on.

Find What You CAN Do

On September 20, 2008 there was a fire at John's house. Rather than a huge blaze, the fire was a slow smolder that began under the deck overnight and didn't become apparent for hours. When John awoke to the smoke and flicker, he stepped out onto his back deck to put out the fire which had essentially become a camouflaged blanket of high-degree, lethal wood. Thank God, only the deck and a little of the house was burnt. However, in the initial seconds, John received third-degree burns on the bottom of his feet, scorching the skin and major nerves that allow us to stand, stabilize, and walk.

To this very moment, John lives in pain. The nerves may or may never regenerate, so John essentially must live with this chronic pain. What percentage of people would be embittered, embattled, and defeated? Who of us would resign to a life of excuses, medication, and anger? John, who loved golf, fishing, and hunting, could no longer do some of the things he used to love.

This is dedicated to my client John.

John decided to focus on what he could do, and made no excuses for what he couldn't. One thing John can do is play water polo. He hadn't played for years prior to the fire, but recently he played in the National Masters tournament. Our lives are filled with reasons not to do something. They may be good reasons, too. But as John's story teaches us, we need to press ahead and find a reason to do what we can.

Most of us can find much smaller reasons not to do something than John has. I want to thank my client and friend, John Nichols, who sustains one of the greatest attitudes towards life I have ever seen.

May it encourage us to abandon our excuses and go be great.

The Great Battle

Two weeks. How many of us have ever begun something new, only to have it start to slip so quickly? How many have stayed steadfast? Why is it so difficult? There is a comfort and predictability to our old habits. Thus, going through this process and staying with a new set of actions requires a tremendous amount of fortitude.

When you run long distances (26.2 miles, for example) there comes a point when just about every cell in your body and mind says "STOP!" There is a real psychological and physiological occurrence (referred to as "the wall") that you must run through if you are going to make the finish line.

The truth is, many don't make it. When you are in pain, and you know that you can end the pain in a second by stopping, it is an unfathomable challenge to keep going.

Habits, disciplines and actions that we committed to just two weeks ago often go by the wayside because in a second we can make a choice to end the pain of change by picking up the cigarette or doughnut or by hitting the snooze button instead of going to the gym.

It is so human to want the comfort back. And yet, if we are to become who we know we can be, we must look at that feeling of comfort like a warrior who sees a great foe... and we must slay it. Most people who make resolutions are neither prepared nor equipped for the battle that lies in front of them — and within them. I believe that you have the courage for the battle, but you must decide whether you want to draw upon that courage or not.

Remember that the battle is won one day at a time.

Just Show Up

Has anyone ever told you that you don't have to be great today? Have you ever had one of "those days" when you can't seem to muster up the inspiration to "finish strong" or "do the impossible" or "crush it?" Not every day can be a personal best. If you think that it should be, your life will be littered with unmet expectations. Most days, just showing up is enough.

Now, that may seem like odd advice coming from a coach whose purpose is to inspire and create change. But in my experience, there are many days in which the inspiration to be excellent just isn't there.

Here's the catch. Do you still show up on those days? Or do you retreat? Believe it or not, beating out the competition sometimes means just showing up when others don't. On those off days, the vast majority of people go into their own private holes. They invent excuses for not being there when they don't "feel like it." Those are the very days when you can gain ground.

There will be other days for taking the hill, conquering the impossible, and shooting for the stars. Most days, you simply need to show up, and do what you do. Undoubtedly this will sound like heresy in the ears of the super-achiever, the individual who believes that winning is all there is. But when you get down to it, that kind of thinking can't be sustained for long, and ultimately leads to burnout.

Today, show up. Make your calls, hit your disciplines, and call it good. There will be plenty of time for an awe-inspiring performance. Today you may win because you simply chose not to back down.

More Courage, Anyone?

I recently read a book in which the authors challenged the validity of the Serenity Prayer:

"God, grant me the Serenity to accept the things I cannot change, the Courage to change the things I can, and the Wisdom to know the difference." This prayer has been a blessing to countless souls over time, and so I was intrigued as to how anyone might challenge its premise. The authors' argument was that too many people looking for "serenity" stopped looking for options and solutions to problems. Their point wasn't that peace and serenity were bad, but rather that many had used it as a way to avoid seeking out and acting with more courage. I thought this was quite a brash statement. But then I considered that we do indeed have the propensity to either overdo or underdo almost anything we endeavor — even the search for peace.

Serenity and peace are, to be sure, great things. But do we act in courage when it is required of us? Do we search for opportunities and solutions to problems? I am sure the answer to these questions will be different for everyone. My prayer for us all is that we would pursue not only serenity, but also courage and wisdom with the same sense of vigor.

In the spirit of Reality and Hope, these are truly dark times for many people — and while peace and serenity is needed, I believe we all need an extra dose of courage to change the things we can. I may even endeavor to expand my thinking on what CAN be changed. That will take courage.

10-1

There's something that has been coming up in coaching which I believe will be instrumental for many of us, and it starts with a silly racquetball analogy. In racquetball, each game is played to 15 points. Sometimes in the course of a match, you are winning a game by the score of 10-1. When this happens, the person who has 10 is actually in a precarious spot — and the person who has 1 knows it.

It is so human to ease up and play lazy when you are winning so convincingly. I can't tell you how many games I have lost because I eased up when I was winning 10-1.

There is a natural human tendency to get complacent when we have achieved some success. You may be in a season where you have some pretty good wind in your sails. If this is the case, the wisest thing you can do is play the game out with excellence. Do not let up. Don't take dumb shots figuring that you are already ahead. Keep making wise decisions.

Life and business have a remarkable way of getting the better of us when we take our eye off the ball. Maybe you have had some success with your health. Maybe you logged a good month or quarter in your business. Maybe you're feeling pretty proud of how far you've come, and that's a good thing. There's nothing wrong with celebrating successes and expressing contentment with life. Just be cautious that it doesn't lead to complacency.

There is a very thin line between contentment and complacency, and when we become complacent, we are on the verge of another tough season. It's a mark of excellence to play the game out and be strong to the final point. By the way, if you feel like you are the person who has a score of 1, isn't it encouraging to know that the odds are still good for you to come from behind and win?

Play all the way through!

Accelerate the Turns

As I look around, I am seeing more and more people waving the white flag. It is commonplace these days to give up on dreams, to stop working on your plans, or to otherwise ease off of a given discipline because you are not getting your desired result. Most people wouldn't have to try very hard to come up with a really good reason to back off.

You could make a list a mile long of reasons to stop trying to be great. And your list would be perfectly justified and brilliantly reasoned. Here's the flaw in your logic: just when there are all these good reasons to back off, there lies an even greater opportunity for those who lean in. When your list of reasons to make a difference dwindles down to just a couple of faint things... this is the time to step on the pedal.

When you're driving into a bend in the road, you don't hit the brakes. You gently accelerate into the turn to preserve your forward momentum. You may not be able to muster up a thousand reasons to go be great today. Maybe you can only come up with one or two. But if that list seems painfully small, please don't forget that it is small for everyone else, too. There is an amazing opportunity for those who will rise up and sink their teeth into the core disciplines they know they should do.

We may be looking back on this time years from now and marveling at the people who created remarkable results because they chose not to participate in backing down or getting by. People who decided to get up and be great anyway. This is the time to step on the pedal. Don't wait until you feel like getting out there. You may not ever feel like it. Accelerate anyway.

JUST HOPE

And in the end, hope wins!

Proof of Hope

Our lives and our businesses move in and out of different seasons. This is dedicated to those who are in the midst of a tumultuous or troubling season right now, who need the hope and belief that their current struggle is a season that will eventually change. Someone once said that in life we are either moving into a crisis, in the middle of one, or coming out of one. Many people struggle with depression, addiction, and other physical or emotional ailments in which they long for hope. Frankly, all too many become hopeless. If you are in a rough season, it can feel impossible to see that there is hope.

But hope exists — and I can prove it.

I have coached some people who have made some subtle changes and have moved out of their difficult season. It can and does happen. People can change. Circumstances do improve.

I point this out because all too often I encounter people who don't see this. Their belief is that we are who we are, and no amount of discipline or action will change things. But if this were true, then there would simply be no books, no stories, no movies or fables about anyone overcoming the odds. These stories resonate with us at a very deep level because we know that something in them is right and therefore possible.

When you hear the "you can do it" message, don't write it off as "rah-rah" malarkey. The fact is that people do overcome challenges, people can change their ways, and rough circumstances will be defeated. If there is a cold hard winter in your life, there must also be a "summer season" coming in which you will experience peace and joy.

If you are in pain, if you are overwhelmed and can't see your way out, if you long to make things different but have lost hope that they ever will be, take heart and take action — things can and do change. It may just have to be you who is the change agent.

Believe and act — in that order.

In the Beginning...

Every December, we participate in an interesting phenomenon. As things slow down a bit, we prepare to ramp up and do it all again for another year — one that we hope will be better than the last. Here we find the true essence of hope: that on the verge of a new year we can reflect and, regardless of how good or bad the previous year was, still believe that the next will bring many great things.

The Apostle Paul says that in the end of times, there will only be three things that last: Faith, Hope and Love. (1 Corinthians 13:13) Much has been written about Love, but there are far fewer words about Faith and Hope.

Faith has been defined as "belief in the unseen." In a way, Hope is the belief in something good in the unseen. That is exactly what we do when we look ahead to the future and predict that good things will come about. We put faith in the goodness of a plan that is unseen.

Strangely, even the worst cynic makes plans for better things. Hopelessness may be the single most crushing feeling one can have. What would our lives look like if we were to wake every day without the hope of something better?

There are people all around the world who live in this reality, and I believe we must pray for them. Beyond our prayers, however, we must endeavor to live in faith. To fully embody our own reality and make plans for hope-filled events. Without Faith and Hope, darkness prevails. We need to bring the light back.

Let us hope for wonderful things ahead. We will continue to embrace reality, but if we are people of the light, then Faith, Hope and Love will shine in and through us.

True Value

For many people, this season is so incredibly hectic, so wrought with doubt and uncertainty, that it can feel as though we are just making it through the days.

We need to remember our worth. Right now, there is a mass of people caught in a cycle of fear, anxiety, and even hopelessness. This is not to say that there aren't some who are doing very well, and who are focused and directed. There are still plenty of these people, and it is my hope that many more can join them — irrespective of what the future throws our way.

I want to lean back towards hope — the kind of hope that is real and not just something we are grasping at falsely. An astute client of mine sent me a quote by French film director and artist Robert Bresson (Roh-bear Bree-sah) and it goes like this:

"Make visible what, without you, might perhaps never have been seen."

Do you realize that you have been given the power to change the world with your words and actions? Is it possible that, from time to time, you have bought the lie that your life doesn't really matter?

Now, certainly there is a way to take this quite narcissistically — I hope that you won't see it that way. From my coach's chair, the broader issue is that too many have stopped believing that what they bring to the table has much worth at all. You have the power to alter human history in a way that no one else can, and you already do it daily. Never forget this. You will destroy many demons if you keep this front and center.

A kind word, a gesture, a simple action can make an eternal difference. Go make the good visible in your vocation and in your life. The world needs to see it!

The Triumph of Hope

There is a story that is embedded deeply into the human heart. It goes something like this...

Once, there was a great and beautiful hope of something to come. There was joyful anticipation of the glory and peace this hope would bring. But then the darkness rose against it. The darkness brought with it despair, anguish, and frustration. The odds were stacked against the original beauty. People began to lose hope, assuming the dark would win.

Then, in a curious twist, a single beam of light broke through. From this single source, hope started to grow, and goodness began its journey back from the depths. But the darkness was powerful, and would not give its ground up easily. After an incredible battle, good triumphed. Hope, peace and love were restored. The evil that once was on top shrank back into a corner... thwarted, but not fully defeated, waiting to return another day.

This is the foundation of many of the movies you have seen and the books you have read. If you look closely enough, you'll see it is also the story of our lives. The question is, where are you in the story? Some of you may be at a point in your story where there is great hope and tremendous peace. For others, you may feel like darkness has conquered and will never give up its ground. I believe there is so much good in seeing the overall story, and knowing that the story plays out over and over again.

There is a reason why stories like *Rocky*, *Star Wars*, *Lord of the Rings* or even *The Notebook* resonate with us. Choose your favorite story and you will probably see something like this pattern emerge. Heck, look in the mirror and you will recognize the story in your own life. There are great battles being fought right now. Are you entrenched in a struggle for your job, your health, or a key relationship? If so, remember this: good wins!

When the battle is raging and hope seems lost, we can forget that good wins out in the end. If you are in a place of hope today, help pull someone else from the mire. The Reality of the Hope to come could be the catalyst for the dawning of a new light.

Thematic Resolve

It seems like everyone has a theory about New Year's Resolutions. Some people make them every year, while others simply refuse because they have given into the futility of them. Then, there are the ubiquitous statistics about what percentage of people actually follow through on their resolutions. I find myself chuckling cynically at how crowded our gym is on January 2nd.

For the record, I have no problem with anyone having a New Year's Resolution. It is my hope that all would go the distance. I have, in the past, made many a resolution of my own... only to see them go by the wayside. This, however, represents the completion of a resolution I made. I resolved that if there were 52 weeks in the year, then I would write 104 times. You are reading the result of that commitment.

I must say that it feels pretty good to stand at the finish line, and I plan on renewing my vow. But now, I want to propose a different type of resolution.

I think it would be great if each of us had a theme for the year. Yeah, I know... specificity is what gets action done. But before we get specific, it is healthy to think about an over-arching theme. Then, we can commit to actions within the backdrop of that theme.

So, what is your theme and what's your resolve? Is it "Restore Physical Health" or "Restore Emotional Health?" Your theme could be personal or professional growth, or building relationships. Regardless of when you are reading this, think of a theme for the year. Then write it somewhere and tell someone. Cheers to your resolve and to your theme. May you be blessed in this next season of your life. Over and out!

Acknowledgments

The obnoxious, invasive elevator music that rushes Academy Award Winners off the stage would long be playing if I were to thank everyone who helped me get *Reality and Hope* to print, let alone getting it to print a second time. If you would like to queue up some music for this, then now's the time.

I do want to thank my colleagues at Building Champions. I spent 13 wonderful years there and without Daniel Harkavy's Vision, I simply would not have had a platform from which to coach. To my fellow coaches at Building Champions, I send special gratitude. Without you, I would have little context for what great coaching is all about. And without the patient endurance of the team at BC, I would have been a lonely lone ranger indeed.

My assistant through those wonderful years was Amy Aamodt-Allenbrand, who graciously oversaw and helped in almost everything I did at work. To Jessica Traffas, my chief editor, who knows my writing as well as anyone and who allowed my voice to happen. To Ryan Lang, who patiently endured my lack of understanding in all things IT.

Thanks to Allie Harkavy for her great eyes in much of the photography. For this second printing, I would like to recognize and thank my colleagues here at Rewire, Inc. In particular, I want to thank Steph Wetherby as she was hugely instrumental in reformatting the book and preparing it for this second printing.

To all of the clients that I have coached and worked with: without you there is no *Reality and Hope* to write. You have inspired me in ways I can't even express. You have shown me an incredible vision of the realness of this world and what is possible.

To Jack Bevilacqua, Kevin Kneafsey, Wil Armstrong, Stacey Harding, and to so many others who speak into my life, I am eternally grateful.

To my unfathomably patient wife, Raffa, and our kids Kelsey, Dayne, Paolo, and Sabrina: you are the greatest blessing a man could receive. Thanking you in the pages of this book does no justice to my true feelings.

Finally, to the God I serve who abides in me: All credit goes to You, for without You I can do nothing. It is my hope that this work honors You.

About the Author

Steve Scanlon is the CEO and Founder of Rewire, Inc, a firm fiercely dedicated to the process of helping organizations and individuals think differently so that they may get authentic, sustainable growth from their work. Steve has accrued more than 14,000 hours of one-on-one work with individuals throughout North America. Prior to launching Rewire, Steve was an executive coach with Building Champions. His consistently full schedule is due to the reputation he has among his clients as a mentor, teacher, and leader with keen discernment, complete honesty, incredible passion, and the courage to ask the right question at the right time. Steve captured many of the lessons from his one-on-one work in writing on his blog entitled *Reality and Hope*, started in January of 2009.

Steve has conducted hundreds of keynote talks, workshops and retreats around the world over the last two decades. He is often sought after to present because of his unique combination of inspiration and action.

Steve and his wife, Raffaella, live in the Portland, Oregon area with their four children: Kelsey, Dayne, Paolo, and Sabrina. He is also the co-founder of the non-profit organization AIM (Avivamiento In Mexico), which supports communities in border towns through providing access to homeownership, education and shelter. He is a passionate runner and marathoner, racquetball player, golfer, fly fisherman, wakeboarder, snowboarder....anything that involves him and his kids playing outdoors in the Pacific Northwest.

CPSIA information can be obtained
at www.ICGtesting.com
Printed in the USA
FSOW01n1456120216
16885FS